TODAY'S AMERICAN HOW FREE?

A FREEDOM HOUSE BOOK

Studies in Freedom

Strategies for the 1980s: Lessons of Cuba, Vietnam, and Afghanistan
Philip van Slyck

Escape to Freedom: The Story of the International Rescue Committee
Aaron Levenstein

Forty Years: A Third World Soldier at the UN
Carlos P. Romulo with Beth Day Romulo

Today's American: How Free?
James Finn & Leonard R. Sussman, (Eds.)

TODAY'S AMERICAN HOW FREE?

EDITED BY
JAMES FINN / LEONARD R. SUSSMAN

FREEDOM HOUSE

Copyright @1986 by Freedom House
Printed in the United States of America. All rights reserved. No part of this book may be used or reproduced in any manner without written permission except in the case of brief quotations embodied in critical articles and reviews. For permission, write to Freedom House, 48 East 21st Street, New York, N.Y. 10010

First published in 1986

Library of Congress Cataloging-in-Publication Data

Today's American.

  (Studies in freedom ; no. 4)
  Includes index.
  1. Civil rights--United States. 2. United States--Politics and government. I. Finn, James, 1924- . II. Sussman, Leonard R. III. Series.
JC599.U5T63 1986   323.4'0973   86-25663
ISBN 0-932088-10-4

Dedication

On the occasion

of the 200th anniversary of the Constitution

and the 45th anniversary of Freedom House

this volume is dedicated to all

    who struggled to establish freedom in this country

    who resisted tyrannies of fascism and communism

    who strive to attain freedom in still oppressive lands

Acknowledgments

Forty-five is only a semiround number, just short of a half-century anniversary. This book's retrospective insights cover four and a half decades because they were, in our view, a historically transitional era (and only secondarily the anniversary of an organization called Freedom House). Following this retrospection the book considers the present and, more important, the future of Americans and their freedoms.

Those forty-five years are demonstrably, however, an era in American history: beginning as America loses its innocence with the bombing of Pearl Harbor, and continuing to today's dawning of a new age, a time still not properly named yet clearly upon us.

These thirteen essays are designed to examine the time ahead, deriving from forty-five years past. With the exception of the editors, the authors are all Trustees of Freedom House. After nearly twenty years' association with

Acknowledgments

this unique band, this writer's admiration for their sophisticated and at times courageous devotion to human freedom increases with each year. It is appropriate, therefore, to acknowledge all the distinguished men and women who guide the policies and programs of Freedom House, together with their associates on the Advisory Council: BOARD OF TRUSTEES: Max M. Kampelman, *Chairman of the Board* (on leave); John W. Riehm, *President*; Bayard Rustin, *Chairman of the Executive Committee*; Leo Cherne, *Honorary Chairman*; Ned W. Bandler, Burns W. Roper, *Vice-Presidents*; Walter J. Schloss, *Treasurer;* Gerald L. Steibel, *Secretary;* Zbigniew Brzezinski, Sol C. Chaikin, Lawrence S. Eagleburger, Richard B. Foster, Richard N. Gardner, Karl G. Harr, Jr., Edmund P. Hennelly, Norman Hill, Sidney Hook, Geri M. Joseph, William R. Kintner, Morton M. Kondracke, Morris I. Leibmen, Charles Morgan, Jr., Daniel P. Moynihan, Albert Shanker, Philip van Slyck, Ben J. Wattenberg, Eugene P. Wigner, Bruce Edward Williams, Jacques D. Wimpfheimer. CHAIR EMERITUS: Margaret Chase Smith. ADVISORY COUNCIL (Domestic): Karl R. Bendetsen, A. Lawrence Chickering, John Diebold, Richard Gambino, Roy M. Goodman, David L. Guyer, Robert Wallace Gilmore, Arthur L. Harckham, Rita E. Hauser, James D. Koerner, Gale W. McGee, Bess Myerson, Whitelaw Reid, Richard R. Salzmann, Robert A. Scalapino, Paul Seabury, Herbert Swope, Robert F. Wagner, Robert C. Weaver. ADVISORY COUNCIL (Foreign): Robert Conquest, *United Kingdom*; Cushrow R. Irani, *India*; Galo Plaza, *Ecuador*; Jean-Francois Revel, *France*; Helen Suzman, *South Africa.*

We acknowledge, too, those on whom our present program builds, departed predecessors of this band, who created and sustained Freedom House for many years:

Acknowledgments

Herbert Agar, Clifford P. Case, Paul H. Douglas, Roscoe Drummond, Father George B. Ford, Thomas K. Finletter, Harry D. Gideonse, Frank Kingdon, Francis Pickens Miller, Robert P. Patterson, Eleanor Roosevelt, Elmo Roper, Whitney North Seymour, Rex Stout, Herbert Bayard Swope, Dorothy Thompson and Wendell L. Willkie. George Field, my predecessor as executive director, midwifed the birth of Freedom House and imaginatively administered its first twenty-five years. The dramatic record of Freedom House's first quarter-century has been faithfully recorded in the 1965 Viking book, *Freedom's Advocate*, by Aaron Levenstein. He died, after long service as a trustee, as *Today's American* was being assembled.

A special acknowledgment goes to each trustee-author for extracting time from busy and productive lives to make possible their contributions. As proof that this book is not a "house" organ, it must accurately be stated that the views expressed by the authors are not necessarily those of Freedom House.

James Finn, the co-editor, has brought to this volume the same insightful judgment and unyielding concern for fact and style that mark his tenure as publications director of Freedom House. We were ably assisted by Mark Wolkenfeld and Jessie Miller.

This book, as I conceived it, seeks to examine the uses and responsibilities of freedom for the benefit of today's and tomorrow's American. That task deserves continuing re-examination.

L. R. S.

Contents

Acknowledgments · vii

Introduction · 1
John W. Riehm

Today's American:
The Complex Challenge · 9
Max M. Kampelman

Mythic Aspects of American Culture · 19
Philip van Slyck

Equal Opportunity
& What's Happened To It · 27
Bayard Rustin

America's Alliances
& The Imperial Conflict · 41
Zbigniew Brzezinski

Academic Freedom:
Problems and Prospects · 55
Sidney Hook

Freedom, Civil Liberties and the Polls · 73
Burns W. Roper

The Press vs. Press Responsibility
in a Pre-Messianic Age 81
Leonard R. Sussman

Computerization and Modern Society 107
John Diebold

**U.S. Intelligence:
Yesterday, Today--and Tomorrow** 115
Leo Cherne

Religion, Morality and Public Values 129
James Finn

**Marxism-Leninism:
Implications for the United States** 145
Paul Seabury

The Promise of National Restoration 161
Morton M. Kondracke

Contributors 171

Index 175

Introduction

John W. Riehm

While the thirteen American Colonies were still years away from independence, the colonists lived in the most democratic society of the eighteenth century. Yet today's Survey of Freedom would rate the colonies only partly free; England was less free; other countries were even more repressive. A survey of comparative civil liberties, telescoping time, would place pre-Revolutionary-War America on a par with Mexico or Taiwan today. Nineteenth-century America provided civil liberties akin to Venezuela, Portugal or India today.

What, then, can be said about today's American--how free is he? How free will he be in the future?

This volume, which marks Freedom House's forty-fifth anniversary, examines the American striving to preserve and expand freedom and democratic values at home and abroad, amid unprecedented technological, social and political change. These essays first probe the complex

Introduction

challenge facing Americans, the real culture they have created, and the problems of equal opportunity at home and an expansive empire abroad. The tensions of a free society--in the universities, the news media, computerization, religion and in intelligence gathering--are examined; so, too, are the implications for Americans of Marxism-Leninism, and, finally, the promise of national restoration.

In the past four and a half decades we have seen great swings between apathy and activism: eras of isolationism, military commitment, an "American Empire," national retreat and national revival. As today's American considers national policies for the immediate future, as well as for the twenty-first century, he should ponder the lessons of the years since World War II.

By October 1941, when Freedom House was created, the democracies of continental Europe had been overrun by the Nazi *blitzkrieg*. The British stood alone embattled on their island, suffering merciless assault by air, awaiting landings by sea.

In America, as in democratic Europe, years of isolationism, bolstered by the USSR's nonaggression treaty with Nazi Germany, and subtle propaganda here and in Europe, had eroded effective resistance by the democracies. Barely three months before Japan's bombing of Hawaii brought the U.S. into the war, renewal of the American military draft passed the House of Representatives by only one vote.

Freedom House was created to help President Roosevelt mobilize American support for the defeated or besieged democrats of Europe and--no less important--"to promote the concrete application of the principles of freedom and democracy," at home and abroad. Wendell L. Willkie, who failed to defeat Roosevelt in 1940, and Mrs. Eleanor Roosevelt, wife of the president, worked together at Freedom House.

Victory over Nazism and fascism did not produce

international peace or even, in many countries, peaceful reconstruction. After 1945, millions of citizens of the Soviet Union died in Communist camps. Today all of Eastern Europe remains under Soviet *diktat*. Scores of former colonial peoples achieved nationhood, but many citizens of the new countries do not enjoy even moderate levels of political rights and civil liberties.

This, in Marxist-Leninist terminology, has produced a "correlation of forces," "coexistence" or "detente." Such "peace" has provided both the opportunity and the facility for Marxist-Leninists to engage in serious ideological warfare by all available means, particularly regional aggression through surrogates. This demonstrates our chief adversary's commitment to sapping the resistance of democratic societies which they regard as preparation for replacing systems founded on individual rights and opportunities with centralized statist controls by governments. Yet for much of that time, Americans understood little of the pervasive quality of Leninist adventurism in both ideology and geopolitics.

The very complexity of underlying issues is bound to generate confusion. Added to that normal complexity, however, are the distortions invented to further confuse fair-minded citizens seeking democratic solutions. One such concoction is the false "balancing" of the values of vastly differing political systems by intentional distortion of the meaning of words.

Too many innocent people seek a good word for the Soviet Union. Their predecessors visited Moscow decades ago and professed to see the wave of the future. After millions of deaths in the Soviet gulags and the continuing obliteration of real dissent, it is difficult to support the Soviet ideological objectives in the United States. It is easier to negate American resistance to those objectives by portraying the American system and the actions of the United States as

Introduction

merely "the other side of the same coin"--the moral equivalent of oppression elsewhere. By such reasoning, the six-year-long Soviet invasion of Afghanistan with 115,000 troops performing horrendous violence that has so far caused nearly 1,000,000 civilian deaths and 5,000,000 others to become refugees, is equated with forty-five United States advisers assisting the elected government of El Salvador to contain a pocket of Marxist insurgents. Such rationalization is specious.

This unthinking support of the Soviet view takes another form. The American commitment to advancing political rights is first denigrated and, when that argument fails, is compared with the supposed Soviet effort to meet human needs (housing, food, health care). Again, this is a false equation. Political rights and civil liberties are the primary key to meeting human needs, as they are to other aspirations. If citizens help choose leaders and policies, they can help decide national priorities, including human needs. Most important, as the Soviet Union has demonstrated for nearly seventy years, societies which deny their citizens political rights and civil liberties do not meet many human needs.

Today, as forty-five years ago, Americans need to understand the way world problems impinge on their personal and national aspirations. Although the communications media deluge us with reports and analyses, and pollsters say Americans know more than they did forty-five years ago, the disinformaton and ideological assaults today are far more subtle and pervasive than in the past. Americans today must be much more sophisticated than in 1941, when resisting Hitler was the primary objective of Freedom House. We must know more about our own society, as well as the challenge from abroad.

Complex constitutional guarantees of personal

4

freedoms, set in law and actively sustained in practice, inevitably generate conflicts of rights. A free press releases limitless kinds of information, some of which may assist potential adversaries of this country, thereby causing officials to withhold such information. Other restrictions on the press stem from rights guaranteed all citizens: the Consitutional pledge of a fair trial to the defendant may be violated by unrestricted coverage by journalists. The press may also be inhibited by the protection provided private citizens from libel or slander. Other clashes of rights arise from the commitment of this society, no longer slaveholding or legally racist, to provide affirmative assistance for blacks without discriminating unfairly against whites who were not themselves guilty of racist practices. Moreover, economic restrictions and corporate regulations to prevent monopolization or unfair business practices properly restrain absolute freedoms.

Such restraints underscore the increasing need in a complex society for journalists, political and corporate leaders and others to act with a sober sense of social responsibility.

Freedom House views its mission for the future as it did in 1941--"to promote the concrete application of the principles of freedom and democracy." In doing so we believe we must try to focus society's attention on what we may call the rule of reason. Far too often, on issue after issue, foreign and domestic, we see the advocates of opposing views becoming overly emotional in their pleading, seeking converts to their cause through an appeal to the emotions rather than through appeal to reason. We view our mission as one of defusing emotion and encouraging constructive dialogue.

Our society faces another dilemma which may be insoluble, but one with which all of us must wrestle if

Introduction

freedom and democracy are to flourish. It is the decline of the balance between the rights of the minority and the will of the majority. It is relatively easy to say the majority rules, but what does that do to an oppressed minority? By the same token one cannot easily speak of "absolute" rights of a minority lest some one or some one group use such rights to intentionally destroy our democratic society.

In a recent address, the Chief Judge of the State of New York, Court of Appeals, Sol Wachtler said: "So long as we recognize that we bear the burden not to appease the majority, but to protect the right of the individual. So long as we are willing to defend in our courts those basic freedoms which are cherished by all of our citizens--even if that protection is unpopular--then we would have done our part in seeing to it that America will survive." Judge Wachtler said this after referring to Thomas Jefferson's statement: "Nothing is unchangeable but the inherent and unchangeable rights of man." Yet in the Freedom House charter reference to "concrete application," how do we balance the different "rights of man"?

The lessons of the first forty-five years of Freedom House should tell us something. We have seen great nonviolent change in civil rights. We went to war in Korea to halt aggression and preserve the fledgling United Nations. We fought another war in Vietnam to an inconclusive end, causing a horrible division in our society. That division raised, in a particular context, the timeless issue of freedom of speech in a democratic society. Freedom House sought to assess objectively the impact of media on the minds of Americans and on the outcome of the war. Out of that effort came the seminal work entitled *Big Story: How the American Press and Television Reported and Interpreted the Crisis of TET 1968 in Vietnam and Washington.*

In 1919 Mr. Justice Holmes, in *Schenck v. United*

States wrote the well known line: "The most stringent protection of free speech would not protect a man in falsely shouting 'fire' in a theater and causing a panic." Subsequently, the view of Mr. Justice Black that freedom of speech was *absolute* came to prevail. The excesses allowed by the application of the Black doctrine, and the growing intolerance of those excesses by the majority of the public, suggest a present shift toward the view of Mr. Justice Holmes. Jurisprudential scholars suggest that this is a reassertion of the "rights vs. duties" philosophy, viz., for every right (freedom of speech) there is a duty (care in the exercise thereof).

We at Freedom House would suggest that society should not ask too much of the law and that a democratic society should not push absolutes too far. Morality and ethics are part of our culture too. Let us recognize and be guided by them. They are not only defenses against the absolute rigidities of communism but directives in the concrete application of the principles of freedom and democracy. Morals and ethics, moreover provide guidance for the rational man against the directives of the demagogue. It is the mission of Freedom House to see that the dialogue of rational man prevails not only for the next forty-five years, but for an indefinite time, in the never-ending search for a freer and more democratic world. To that end we dedicate this volume.

Today's American:
The Complex Challenge

Max M. Kampelman

It's a complex fate, being an American." This was true when Henry James first stated it more than one hundred years ago. In a sense, it is no less true today, although in this period the element of "complex challenge" appears to be dominant.

From the time of the founding of this country, the fate of the American has been both complex and changing. I need go no further back than to the beginning of Freedom House, forty-five years ago, to show how rapidly some of these changes occur. Freedom House was established in New York five weeks before United States forces were attacked at Pearl Harbor. For many months before that our country was sharply divided in a fierce, internal struggle to decide which of two conflicting strains in our short history would dominate. The forces of isolationism and pacifism were pitted against those of internationalism and intervention. As the Axis forces extended their military victories, a number of

Today's American

civic leaders who argued for more direct U.S. engagement joined forces to proclaim a "two-fold fight for freedom"-- against totalitarianism abroad and for freedom at home. The national debate over whether to intervene militarily against the Axis powers was settled decisively at Pearl Harbor on 7 December 1941. The considered opinion of Freedom House, and large numbers of other people, became the consensus of the country. The United States became an active participant in a war fought on either side of the globe.

* * *

Before the war, the United States was one among the nations of the West. After 1945, when the war ended, the United States emerged as the natural leader of nations that were materially, emotionally and, in some instances, morally exhausted. Before the war, our nation was innocent of atomic power; after the war, we not only had the knowledge and technology necessary to split the atom, to create fission, but knowledge of the tremendous destruction the atomic bomb could release. Before the war, pacifists could assert that "the power of love and nonviolence" could overcome the evils of totalitarianism; after the war, with the impersonalized nature of nuclear war, that illusion disappeared. During the war, we were allied with the Soviet Union to defeat the Axis powers; after the war, our nation came again gradually to recognize the expansive totalitarianism of the Soviet Union, and that the containment of that expansion posed a challenge to the United States and its allies. Before the war, the colonial powers still exercised substantial hegemonies; after the war, this power declined and many new nations came into existence. Before the war there were strong differences between nationalists who put their faith in the system of sovereignty that prevailed and internationalists who looked toward international organizations endowed with sufficient authority and force to ensure peace among nations. The war did not resolve these differences. Nevertheless, there was early consensus that the United States should work to make the United Nations a success.

Much of what we Americans must cope with today is a legacy of that earlier period: more than a hundred new nations and shifting alliances; a militarily strong, aggressive and expansive Soviet Union; an unsatisfactory equilibrium based on a nuclear deterrent system; "Third World" countries whose actions often belie their democratic rhetoric; an accelerating technology that has not only affected our military forces but has revolutionized the process of communication; and a U.N. that has revealed all too starkly an inability to fulfill the high hopes with which it was originally invested.

To these factors must be added a more explicit and developed national concern with human rights and a stronger focus on international economic issues. The United States must deal with both rich and poor countries in a context in which free enterprise is often under attack; and when national leaders of many countries, including our own, sometimes speak as if global economics were a zero-sum game--"You are rich because you took from the poor; we are poor because you are rich." This erroneous belief is so widespread and firmly entrenched that it will not soon be dissipated. Both by precept and example we must show that it is wrong, that free enterprise, as an essential aspect of democratic capitalism, promotes economic growth and encourages freedom. Recent studies have shown a high correlation between economic growth and political rights. It is part of our present task to show that this correlation, though not inevitable, is not accidental; that it is out of concern for both the material well-being and the political freedoms of other peoples that we uphold free enterprise and democracy and oppose collectivisms that unite political and economic leadership in one state-controlled office.

We must cope with all these issues on an international level even as much of our attention is turned inward. We have, for example, made advances from the early days of Freedom House when our trustee Wendell L. Willkie attacked racial segregation in the armed forces; and when that attack was broadened into a call for equal opportunity and treatment for black workers. But much remains to be done. At a time of vast technological and economic shifts, worldwide, we must create many new jobs. We must do this even as we incorporate into our society increasing numbers of people from Third World countries. We must also build into our system still stronger shields for our citizens against the worst onslaughts of poverty and sickness.

* * *

Given the responsibilities that are ours as a great nation and given our admitttedly great resources, what is the proper role of the United States? What are the choices open to us? How free are we to determine our own destiny and to help other countries shape theirs?

In sketching in some of the contours of the world scene, and America as part of that scene, we cannot ignore the element of change, which is both a most noticeable and potentially exciting feature. However, there is also a necessary and welcome element of stability in our political affairs, both domestic and international. As a nation we have gone through wrenching periods when it seemed as if internal divisive forces would tear us apart. But we have, finally, held together. We now recognize that there is more that unites the majority of the citizens of the United States than divides us. This will remain true even as new waves of immigrants change our national makeup. But this is a truth that does not go unchallenged, either in theory or practice. There are in our society today, as there have been in our past, ideologues on the extreme left and the extreme right who, in the name of their parochial certitudes, would impose their values on the majority of their fellow citizens. There are groups that, fearing the future, would hold fast to the patterns of the past even as the forces of change are transforming the world around them. Others, regretting only that the changes are too slow, would jettison practices and institutions that both moderate those changes and winnow them out, separating the desirable from the undesirable. It has been the genius of our political system to preserve the institutions that our realistic forebears have bequeathed to us even as we use them creatively to facilitate change, to adapt to new conditions.

I do not mean to describe ours as a smooth and untroubled political system, a genteel procedure. It is not that. There is much room in our system, frequently oversubscribed, for the rough and tumble, for fierce and even abrasive debate. But our tradition asserts that when that debate passes through our legislative, executive and judicial processes, the debate is, for the time, settled. Those who are unhappy with the decision may continue to oppose it. The debate may be reopened at another time. But the basis of our political system and our society is threatened when that decision is challenged not by further debate but by violence, fear and coercion, weapons wielded by ideologues who place the merits of their political position over those of the democratic process. There are both idealogues and antidemocratic forces in our society today. We can best

Today's American

ensure their isolation by guaranteeing that the rest of our citizens can participate in and benefit from the democratic process.

It does not diminish our domestic problems, or the necessity to address them, to say that it is the antidemocratic forces abroad that most threaten our society and its values. The most obvious manifestation of this threat is, of course, the Soviet Union. The combination of its great military strength, its totalitarian ideology and policies, its expansionist history, its proclaimed intentions--all of these pose a threat of formidable dimensions. That threat is sometimes obscured or camouflaged by the Soviet's rhetorical devotion to peace, to democracy, to progressive change. But intermittently the reality breaks through and we see naked the aggressive power that has even recently extended itself in Poland, Afghanistan, Latin America, Africa--in fact, in every continent except North America. The Soviet threat, it is clear, is directed not only at the United States. It is directed at other free countries, and at many countries whose people aspire to greater independence and freedom. The United States is not free to disregard or minimize that threat. If we value freedom itself, we are free only to challenge and counter it.

* * *

The gulf between the Soviet Union and the United States is profound. Our political systems, our values, our cultures are different. We differ in how we regard our own citizens and those of other countries. We differ in our worldviews. We differ in how we believe change should occur both within and between our societies and theirs, between free societies and totalitarian societies. Change is inevitable; it will come. But we do not believe that violence is necessary to midwife its arrival. We believe that desirable change can be peaceful. We have been taught by the Soviet Union and its leaders that they do not share that belief. No bridge thrown over the gulf of these present differences will minimize them. Nevertheless, the bridge of dialogue and negotiations must be maintained, as it has been, for example, in cultural affairs, in economic matters, in arms negotiations and in the Helsinki process. Even as we negotiate we must remain keenly aware of the differences. We must remain aware of them and the specific problems that flow from them if we are to summon up the strength and perseverance to cope with them adequately. If we are to preserve peace, avoid falling into unprecedented destruction, we will need all the resources a strong democracy can provide.

One of the most profound commentators on American life pointed out early in the last century that the democratic virtues so beneficial to the arrangement of our domestic life were not necessarily those most suited to the management of foreign affairs. Alexis de Tocqueville noted that free and open debate, free and frequent elections with the subsequent change of government leaders, the disclosure of state affairs--these were not conducive to a foreign policy designed for the long haul. Yet, in the face of a long-standing recognizable threat, steadiness, stability and perseverence are what we need. The polarities and divisiveness of partisan policies, highly familiar to us in domestic affairs, are a luxury in foreign affairs, a luxury that even a very strong, rich country can ill afford. We must develop within acceptable boundaries of criticism and free debate a common stance on questions vital to our national security. A democracy cannot command unity, as a totalitarian country can, but it can inspire it. In the long run, an inspired and educated citizenry is both stronger and more

Today's American

flexible than one that is commanded. We will differ--we do differ--on matters of national defense. But it should not be impossible to agree that our defense should be designed to avoid nuclear escalation, to deter aggression, to maintain national security, to discourage coercion--and to keep the debate within these boundaries. This is not an easy task. De Tocqueville's insight into the relation between democratic procedures and foreign policy finds ready support in our recent history. If we are to develop a united and determined opposition to the forces that threaten freedom today, if we are to shape a durable foreign policy, we must acknowledge that what is not an easy task is simply a necessary task.

* * *

Both critics and supporters of the United States often refer to its vast resources and its corresponding responsibilities. These help to define its proper role in world affairs today. That definition is not complete, however, without reference to our limitations. We did not seek world leadership and we are still uncomfortable with it. Shortly after World War II, this country passed through a short and heady period when some national leaders in different fields spoke as if, on the international scene, we were omnipotent, invulnerable, unchallengeable. This was hubris of a high order. We are none of these things. We are far from being omnipotent. There are vast problems in the world that we did not cause and which we are powerless to resolve. (It is, in fact, more realistic to speak of some trying world situations not as problems--which implies that there are solutions--but as conditions, which will change in time in ways that we cannot now foresee.)

We are not invulnerable, nor is any country in a world armed with nuclear weapons. Our military and our economic strength have fluctuated relative to that of both friendly and hostile nations. Neither are we completely shielded from the impact of great economic shifts, as both the oil crisis and the impressive economic performance of Japan have confirmed. We are not unchallengeable, as both individual and state terrorism have revealed to all observers. We have responsibilities, but they are not indefinite. We have great resources, but they are not inexhaustable. There are limitations to our power, to our reach. If we are to preserve our freedom and help others maintain or achieve theirs, we must be clear about what we can do and what we can't do as a nation, what we should do and what we should not attempt. As always those are easier to state in the generality than to decide in the particular. But the generalization will provide the guidelines.

It is a classic statement of national interest to say that we should provide for the well-being of our citizens and guard them from external attack. This is not, as some have misinterpreted it, a call for isolation or for withdrawing from international affairs. A moment's thought should make evident that we could accomplish neither of the two stated goals of our national purpose if we attempted to withdraw into "fortress America." A clear statement of our national interest is a call, rather, for continuing assessment, within broad policy outlines, of our domestic life and of our relations with our allies and other countries.

* * *

I stated earlier that change is inevitable. In fact, change is a constant in domestic and international life as it is in our personal lives. Some years back the United States was the unquestioned center of scientific and technological advance. We are still such a center, but now there are other

Today's American

contenders. And some of them are our allies. Even as we welcome their advances, their increased economic weight, we must strive to keep a cutting edge in the rapidly accelerating world of high technology, or we will surely fall behind. We should also recognize that these changes affect not only our domestic life and our international economic relations. They also affect the nature of our strategic and tactical forces. With increased material and economic strength, allied countries take on increased military responsibilities. Put simply, in terms of our national interest the United States should not expend its resources on efforts that other countries can and should make for themselves. This still leaves a very large area for negotiation, for different evaluations of both strengths and responsibilities, for needed mutual cooperation.

Applied consistently, this criterion will enable us to retain and extend our own freedoms at home, to succor and support similar freedoms abroad, to show by word and deed that such freedoms are the right and can be the goal of peoples in all corners of the globe.

How free, then, is today's American?

Since individual freedom guarantees the right and opportunity to make real choices--for one's own life, and the leadership and policies of one's country--today's American is the freest person ever, here or elsewhere. He is particularly free to help remove the still substantial hindrances to a "more perfect union."

Mythic Aspects of American Culture

Philip van Slyck

Condescension toward American "culture" and the dominant values of American civilization is hardly new. It did not begin with the capture by Hollywood of the twentieth century's only original art form, film. Nor did it start with the so-called youth rebellion of the 1960s and 70s, and the advent of hard rock, long hair and the subculture of drugs and promiscuity. Cultural self-deprecation has been faddish among worldly wise Americans, at least since the early nineteenth century. Critics, indigenous and foreign, found American arts, literature and lifestyles quaint, bumptious and generally inferior to older and more sophisticated traditions from which Americans had borrowed indiscriminately without--it was said--establishing a legitimate national culture of their own.

Moreover, the deficiencies of this *noveau* civilization were viewed by some as inherent in the demography and politics of the first society in history that had, in effect,

American Culture

invented itself. Alexis de Tocqueville, surely the friendliest of foreign critics of American democracy, warned in the 1830s that democratic egalitarianism is susceptible to excesses, lending itself to a tyranny of the majority, to an overblown individualism that is indifferent to the broader interests of the society, and to a single-minded pursuit of materialist success. American liberty, he cautioned, should be wary of being reduced to a "private free-for-all, loser beware."

Yet one of the most frequent criticisms of American society is that it is excessively materialistic. Throughout the first half of this century, a recurring theme in American literature and political philosophy was the polyglot character of popular American culture, and the consequent difficulties in transcending this turbulent interaction of ethnic and racial diversities, and continent-wide regional differences, to create a cultural union with something of value to offer the rest of the world. The sheer vitality of pluralist American society was often read as a cultural flaw. Social critics such as Upton Sinclair, Sinclair Lewis and H.L. Mencken satirized the rags-to-riches materialism of, say, the fictional George Babbitt, who "was nimble in the calling of selling houses for more than people could afford to pay." Yet opportunity for the nimble was and still is a mythic source of optimism for successive generations of immigrants from old worlds to the new.

* * *

As the United States emerged in midcentury as the world's dominant and most energetic economic, military and political power, both domestic and foreign perceptions of the potency of American culture began to alter significantly. In a world faced with the formidable tasks of postwar reconstruction and decolonization, and threatened by aggressive Communist expansion into Central Europe and the Far East, the validity of American cultural values was no longer a domestic parlor game of only passive intellectual interest to the rest of the world. The competence of America to provide global leadership in keeping the peace and stabilizing world order suddenly became the concern of all who looked to America for support, protection or favor.

The generous American response to international expectations in the immediate postwar era put a burnish of the idealistic onto American materialism. If the business of America was business, and its ultimate goal was material success, so be it: out of enlightened self-interest, these American assets were being mobilized to contain Communist expansion, to rebuild war-torn Europe and to launch international economic development and trade expansion on a scale never before attempted. If American civilization lacked the subtlety and polish of the *anciens regimes*, it had also avoided their decadence and failures. With the collapse of the old empires, America offered the fresh vision of a pluralist world order based on self-determination and the spread of democratic insititutions--an extension of its own domestic vision.

The progress has been slow, uneven, often sidetracked and in places fiercely resisted, especially by powerful antidemocratic adversaries, but also at times by undemocratic "friends," reluctant to give up personal power. Even so, the vision of a pluralist and open world order, hospitable to freedom, remains one of the most powerful ideas in international relations, and democratic aspirations continue to animate the politics of modernizing nations from Argentina and Brazil to the Philippines and the Republic of Korea. Throughout the postwar era, under leadership of both parties, U.S. foreign policy has generally sought to advance these goals--sometimes ineptly, sometimes tardily and occasionally unsuccessfully but on balance it has done so to the credit of the American people and their public philosophy.

Surely it was no coincidence that, in those early years of American ascendancy to international leadership, historic transformations were undertaken in the moral foundations of American society--most notably, the progressive dismantling since the 1950s of the legal framework for racial segregation, and corresponding advances in civil rights legislation. Those domestic reforms, which purged centuries of government condonation of cultural bigotry, also laid the groundwork for successive U.S. administrations, since the 1960s, to embrace the cause of human rights in the world.

* * *

Despite this progress, the self-derogation of American cultural values did not go out of fashion. On the contrary, events of the 1960s and 70s ushered in a crisis of beliefs whose residue still litters American society. The so-called youth rebellion of the 60s and early 70s, with its emblems of frenetic music, counterculture lifestyles and dress and rejection of institutional authority, peaked in the late 60s when the militant antiwar movement indulged in violent assaults on university administrations, political conventions and the Pentagon.

This upheaval by what Chief Justice-designate Rhenquist has called "the new barbarians" succeeded in polarizing the society, not solely on the merits or demerits of their cause, but also because of their alliance of convenience with other popular discontents--in particular the nonviolent civil rights movement, which was also challenging the status quo for minorities and the poor in political, educational and

van Slyck

job opportunities and social services. The crisis only deepened with the mindless political assassinations of 1968, the rapid erosion of political support for the attenuated Vietnam war and the national humiliation of Watergate.

Healing was slow, and the polarization has in some respects hardened, but popular morale and self-confidence have largely been restored under new leadership in the 80s. Vietnam and Watergate are behind us, the rebellious generation of the 60s is busy making a living and the current college generation appears to be preparing itself for Wall Street. Yet the widening gap between haves and have-nots-- and the actual or threatened dismantling of welfare programs and civil rights protection--leaves a considerable body of unaddressed discontent. The Reagan Administration, with support of a substantial popular majority, has achieved a radical alteration of national priorities--guns and butter, on credit, with nothing to spare for social reform. The terms liberal and conservative have been assigned new meaning in the ideological marketplace, and only time will tell if the nation's new directions--whether described as a reversion to social Darwinism or an opening to a bright new era for all-- are irreversible.

There are ironies in the current national ebullience, and the skills with which it has been engineered. Not too long ago, the shallowness of America's cultural impact on the rest of the world was often summed up in two examples: Hollywood films (then as now our most visible cultural export) and the advertising-public relations industry. The belittling of American film output is no longer persuasive. Indeed, in film as well as the other arts, Americans today rank among the most creative contributors to international culture. Yet the images of Hollywood and Madison Avenue hype, make-believe, and the exploitation and manipulation of gullible masses still lurk in the cultural memory. The irony is

American Culture

that a Grade B movie actor of a bygone era has turned out to be a Grade A political leader, whose communications skills have been at least as important as his policies in restoring popular morale and reasserting America's international leadership, after a prolonged period of national malaise and self-doubt.

* * *

    In this and other ways, the American presence in the postwar world has profoundly affected the values of other peoples and the dynamics of the international community. The evolving (and increasingly interdependent) world political economy, for example, has served as proving ground for the typically (but hardly exclusive) American belief in the productive power of private enterprise, operating in free markets, with a minimum of government intervention aside from reasons of public health and safety and the preservation of competition. This traditional belief has been refurbished and nurtured under the Reagan administration, with no small impact in the world economy. In Western Europe and most of the high-growth newly industrializing nations of Pacific Asia and Latin America, recent policy is also moving in the direction of freer, less-regulated markets and, in several cases, the privatization of industries that had earlier been socialized.

    America did not invent laissez-faire economics, but in the past forty years the business-oriented American culture brought the mixed-market economy to a degree of refinement that has made it an acknowledged if imperfect model for developed and developing economies alike. Even China and several Eastern European states are experimenting with free markets within their centrally planned economies. Indeed, although the U.S. economy has, for the past four years, been operating "out of sync" with most of its trading partners, and is now burdened with the greatest budget, trade and payments deficits of any nation in history, the rest of the world continues to imitate the American model for want of a better alternative.

In part because of the scale of the American presence in the world, it has become less fashionable these days for America's friends abroad to dismiss or pick fault with American culture--certainly not in the artistic realm, nor even in the realm of traditional American values. The worries and complaints focus more on transient policies, or the seeming absence of policies, and on means rather that ends. What America *does* is watched carefully around the world because America's policies and performance are integral and potentially decisive to the flow of history.

Perhaps to a greater extent than ever before, the diverse and dynamic American culture is acknowledged as a mature and shaping force in an emerging global civilization. In this perspective, even the contradictions, crassness and shallowness of America have their tolerable place. The failings are human and universal, not peculiar to America.

It is still difficult for members of more homogeneous and traditionalist societies to understand the extraordinary diversity of American demography. Indeed, it is proving difficult for some second-generation Americans to accept the inflow and quick success of highly motivated new Americans from unfamiliar places, such as Vietnam and Cambodia. Yet the society of immigrants continues to function reasonably well, as it did when de Tocqueville first assayed it, and that reality is the justification as well as the promise of the continuing American experiment in pluralist democracy.

Equal Opportunity & What's Happened To It

Bayard Rustin

In an industrial democracy, the concept of freedom of opportunity is predicated on two basic principles: 1) that the economic system can provide *opportunity* for social and economic progress to all those willing to work; and 2) that it is the duty of government to guarantee all its citizens *equal* access to the avenues of progress. Today, profound structural changes in the economy and a national social policy that absolves government of its traditional role as overseer of the general welfare have seriously eroded these twin pillars of economic and social justice, particularly for blacks, women and other minorities.

On the economic front, rapid de-industrialization, the advent of technological innovations such as automation and robotics, the loss of millions of manufacturing jobs, have led to declining opportunity for large segments of the working class. And while blacks have been disproportionately hurt by

Equal Opportunity

these developments--and are perhaps their most conspicuous victims--attendant problems such as unemployment, poverty, inadequate housing and family dissolution, are steadily permeating large sectors of society, from the depressed farmbelt to the ravaged industrial centers of this nation.

In the realm of social policy, the government's avowed commitment to a free-market philosophy has resulted in a marked reluctance to enforce civil rights provisions and implement programs to alleviate the problems of those Americans hardest hit by the changing economic landscape--the unemployed, the under-trained, the poor. The Reagan Administration's continuing assault on affirmative action, voting rights laws and equal education, social assistance and employment-training programs threatens to undermine decades of economic and social progress by blacks, women and other minorities.

Clear barometers of the deteriorating economic opportunities for blacks are the general worsening of the labor market position for blacks during the past five years and the persistent growth of the urban underclass. But while the solutions to these problems are essentially nonracial (they depend on the overall improvement of the national economy), the precariousness of black inroads into the economic mainstream, attributable to decades of discrimination and inequality, and the particular nature of the black experience, calls for special analysis.

* * *

The watershed of the black struggle for equal opportunity was marked by the sweeping civil rights legislation of the 1960s. Perhaps the most noteworthy characteristic of the black agenda through the early 60s was its simplicity. The issue was the straightforward imperative to overcome racist barriers to normal participation in American society: the right to vote, the right to attend public schools regardless of race, full access to public accommodation. With the exception of hardcore racists and a handful of doctrinaire segregationists, there was little disagreement with the principle that the federal government had a moral obligation to tear down those barriers, even if doing so required expanded government activism.

In addition to the moral force generated by the civil rights movement, the black community benefited from the fact that its demands asked little of the American people in economic terms. The adoption of the most sweeping laws presented no challenge to the economic system or its well-being. With the exception of the minimal cost of establishing civil rights enforcement mechanisms, the demands of the movement cost the taxpayer very little indeed. Even the subsequent antipoverty and social programs of the Great Society were relatively inexpensive given the overall robustness of the economy.

The successes of the civil rights movement in its first decade can be attributed to a unique confluence of social and economic factors. The establishment of the legal foundation of civil rights, which provided access to political power and, in terms of human dignity, enhanced the lives of millions of blacks, came at a time when America enjoyed a period of prosperity approaching full employment and sustained growth in manufacturing and other basic industries.

The enactment of civil rights legislation also led to social mobility. Until the 60s, urban blacks of all classes were largely confined to ghettos, which had their own class structure. Outside the ghetto, a highly educated black had virtually the same social status as a black field hand. South of Washington D.C., Ralph Bunche and a sharecropper were treated the same. With the advent of the civil rights

Equal Opportunity

laws, upper and middle class blacks, in their new-found freedom, moved steadily out of the ghettos into the newly integrated society, leaving behind the poor, the underclass. Paradoxically, this new mobility was at least partly responsible for the decline of the inner city schools, housing and religious institutions. Black hotels, first-class restaurants, theaters and retail stores virtually disappeared from the ghettos.

* * *

After the hard-fought legal and judicial struggle of the mid-1960s, blacks now faced the challenge of gaining political power and economic stability, which meant greater integration into the economic mainstream. But just as most whites in American society were now prepared to accept blacks, shifting political and economic trends posed new obstacles.

As blacks began to flex their political muscle in the late 60s, the economic boom was giving way to serious changes in America's economic landscape that were to be severely crippling in the 70s. The economy, primed by the Vietnam war, was begining to falter. By the mid-70s, the nation was facing high inflation, exorbitant interest rates, shifting trade patterns and sluggish growth. In addition, labor-intensive industries, long a primary vehicle for black economic advancement, not only began to decline at home, but also began to move rapidly overseas. Semiskilled and unskilled workers, many of them black, were displaced as a consequence of cybernation and other technological advances. As manufacturing businesses declined or moved out of the northern and midwestern industrial centers, blacks who migrated from the south in the 50s to seek greater economic opportunity found themselves both unable to compete for jobs in the growing high-tech, financial and service sectors, and also unable to relocate.

This increase in male joblessness, and its effect on the stability of the black family, coupled with the failure of government programs to stem such social deterioration in the black community caused by displacement and decades of discrimination, contributed to the growth of the black underclass, especially in the inner cities. A bitter irony of these developments was that blacks were increasingly capturing political power in an institution--the urban political machine--at a time when large cities were in economic and social recession. This compounded frustration led to hopelessness and despair, and further deterioration of the black family.

To further add to the dilemma, the national political climate began to shift. The tide of political and fiscal conservatism that ushered in the 80s was based on a philosophy that absolved government of its social responsibilities and blindly sought to apply marketplace solutions to the country's growing economic woes. Moreover, the public sector, which in recent years employed some 60 percent of all black college graduates, began to decline, with adverse ramifications for the black middle class. The continued erosion of America's industrial base had a devastating impact on the black working class. And cutbacks in social assistance further undermined the social fabric of the already hard-pressed underclass.

Because black economic progress is intimately linked to the economic health of the nation, increasing economic difficulties of blacks are linked to the general failure of the economy to perform well for American workers in general, particularly in the last six years. Hence while racial discrimination continues to be a factor in black economic and social progress, the sustained improvement in the economic

Equal Opportunity

conditions of the blacks depends primarily on improving the overall performance of the economy. Despite the Administration's continued claims of economic recovery, today's economy is plagued by high unemployment, wage stagnation, sluggish job growth, declining purchasing power, high trade and budget deficits, low savings rates and deflation, which cripple the goods-producing sector. While these conditions have led to an ever-increasing number of poor, blacks *and* whites, blacks have been especially hard hit.

Poverty and unemployment rates for blacks are at their highest levels of the post-1964 period. Black wages continue to be low, absolutely and relative to white wage rates, and the gap is widening. The median weekly earnings for full-time black workers fell from $279 in 1979 to $267 in the first quarters of 1985. In 1985, a staggering 34 percent of blacks were living in poverty, compared to 12 percent of whites. The figure is higher than it has been in any of the 10 years preceding the Reagan Administration. Over 51 percent of all black children are poor, the highest figure since the government started recording statistics in 1970. Even more disturbing, 66.2 percent of all black children living in female-headed households were poor in 1984. The black unemployment rate stands about 15 percent, and the rate for black teenagers is a staggering 40 percent.

* * *

A major factor in these bleak statistics is the changing face of the American economy. Since 1980, America has lost 2.5 million factory jobs. Another 200,000 in the auto industry have disappeared, and still an additional 200,000 in textiles and 200,000 more in electronics. All the job growth in manufacturing which occurred in the 60s and 70s has been lost in the first half of the 80s. In 1970, manufacturing accounted for 33 percent of all private jobs. By 1985, that number had plummeted to 23.8 percent.

The loss of these high-paying, mostly unionized jobs has had a deleterious impact upon all workers, but blacks--particularly men--have been especially affected. Some 60 percent of black male workers with "middle-class" earnings work, not as white-collar professionals, but as semiskilled operatives or in construction-labor jobs. In addition, the employment status and prospects of blacks and other minorities have been further limited by the American economy's deteriorating international position, which has been exacerbated by unfair foreign competition, misguided trade policies and, until recently, the high value of the dollar. Nonwhite workers are largely concentrated in the lower-paying, blue-collar occupations, and thus are disproportionately harmed by fluctuations in foreign trade.

The steady and deep decline in basic industries has also been accompanied by a drop in public sector jobs. The budget-slashing fervor gripping federal, state and municipal agencies threatens to undermine black employment gains in this sector. Some 23 percent of all male workers are in government jobs, as are 34 percent of black male managers and 52 percent of all black male professionals. A high percentage of black women also work in the public sector.

Yet another critical factor contributing to the decline in black economic progress is the increase in the number of people seeking jobs and the expansion of the nonindustrial, service sector of the economy, which has traditionally been largely nonunionized and lower-paying. Since 1972, the proportion of the population participating in the civilian workforce has increased from 60.4 to 64.4 percent, with a dramatic influx of women. The resulting job shortage has had a severe impact on blacks trying to find work,

Equal Opportunity

particularly men. In addition, job growth has shifted away from the high-paying, goods-producing industries to the lower-paying service, finance and trade sectors. Between 1981 and 1985, more than 6.8 million private sector jobs were added in the nongoods-producing sectors. In 1970, for example, the retail trade and service sectors together accounted for about 38.7 percent of all jobs. By 1985 their share of private sector jobs had increased to 48.2 percent.

Of particular concern to black male workers is that the sectors that have been growing more rapidly have traditionally employed more women than men. In retail-trade, 52.2 percent of all workers are women; in real estate, 57.7 percent; and in services, 60.7 percent. Moreover, the sectors in which most job growth is occurring are also the lowest wage sectors. In 1984, for instance, the usual weekly earnings for full-time workers in manufacturing was $373, compared to a mere $176 for retail workers and $249 for workers in services. These low wage rates also have had an impact on the economic status of women in these sectors, particularly those who are heads of households.

The coming together of these trends--a low-growth economy, a decline in basic industries and technological displacements, the growth of low-wage, nonunion sectors of the economy--has contributed to the skyrocketing unemployment rate for black men and women, and to a decline in real wage rates and earning power. In turn, male joblessness has contributed to the deterioration of the black family, a rapid increase in female-headed households, and the expansion of the underclass.

* * *

No discussion of the decline in economic opportunities for blacks is complete without some analysis of the black underclass. No other segment of the black community has generated so much anguish, internal debate and controversy in political and academic circles. The statistics illuminating the problems of the underclass are disturbing. The percentage of black families headed by women is estimated to be nearly 50 percent, and well over that in urban areas. Black births outside of marriage are now over 58 percent, compared to 12 percent for whites. In crime-ridden ghettos, the leading cause of death for young black males is homicide. A recent survey found that crime, predominantly committed against other blacks may account for more than 25 percent of black teenage income in inner cities.

It has been suggested that the problems of the black underclass are rooted in a social pathology spawned by years of welfare dependence. Others believe that the breakdown of traditional values, the declining role of religion, and the personal dislocation are partly the result of the rapid migration of blacks from the rural South to the northern cities. Another contributing factor is the flight of the black elite from the inner urban areas.

Yet what needs to be stressed is that the problems of the black underclass families are not the problems of blacks, but problems of the poor. In the depressed industrial areas of northern England, for example, illegitimacy, family dissolution, single-parent households, teenage pregnancy, all are rampant. The problems of the black underclass are thus clearly the problems of the poor working class; they are economic and not racial. For instance, middle- and upper-class blacks, like their white counterparts, are more likely to live in two-parent households and have small families, and are not plagued by the pathology of the black poor family. The key to improving the nature of the distressed black family, then, is upward economic mobility.

Equal Opportunity

So what is to be done to enhance equal opportunity for blacks? Affirmative action, while enhancing prospects for some, has its limitations for it can only apply where jobs exist. Clearly, today's black agenda must be part of an agenda for all Americans. It must be a plan for economic prosperity and growth reaffirming the notion that social policy is the legislative and administrative law aimed at reducing poverty, broadening economic opportunities and protecting basic rights. Such an agenda should include the following:

*A national commitment to protect and expand basic industries, with increased investment in goods-producing and manufacturing sectors. A national industrial policy must make it a top priority to save beleagured American industries from unfair competition by adopting equitable trade policies, while discouraging business from relocating abroad.

*A national commitment to excellence in education and to federal programs in vocational and job-training to help blacks and others enter an increasingly specialized and competitive job market. The American economy is no longer a system where the poor and the uneducated can sell the only commodity they have--muscle power. The government must play an active role in easing the transition of workers displaced by cybernation and other technological advances, and in developing a more highly skilled workforce able to compete in the international marketplace. Modernization in the ways that goods are produced and distributed is both necessary and desirable in today's world. The issue is the failure to readjust to it. There must be a unified effort by business, trade unions and government to retrain workers and to sustain them at a just economic rate during that retraining. Those who argue that such programs would be expensive must realize that for every one million people unemployed, the cost to the U.S. is a staggering $24 billion annually in lost federal taxes (both business and individual), a figure that does not include the revenues lost to states and cities.

The education agenda must also include sweeping public school reforms such as those put forth in the Carnegie report, *A Nation Prepared: Teachers for the 21st Century*, and endorsed by American Federation of Teachers' President Albert Shanker. The report advocates higher standards for teachers, the creation of a national board of outstanding teachers to set standards for the profession, and the expanded use of computers and other state-of-the-art technology to free teachers to coach students in such skills as thinking, reading and writing. Public education must be upgraded to meet the needs of the changing economy and other societal changes.

The government should also insure affordable education for qualified individuals who do not have the means to pay the ever increasing tuition rates. Since we no longer have land-grant colleges and cheap state or city schools where immigrants and the poor used to get an affordable education, many no longer have access to a higher education.

*A national commitment to formulate and implement a strategy for reducing poverty and easing the suffering of the underclass. There must be a renewed commitment to social spending for the poor and ill-trained to help break the cycle of joblessness, poverty and crime that threatens a growing segment of our society. The government must provide access to certain essential services for the elderly, the destitute and the unemployed. We must accept the obvious fact that there are many among the poor who are simply psychologically unequipped to cope with the harsh realities thrust upon them by urban life. Of course these programs will be costly. In the long term, however, they will be less

Equal Opportunity

expensive for society than keeping people in jails, mental institutions and drug rehabilitation centers.

*A national commitment to safeguarding civil rights and antidiscrimination laws and regulations that have been indispensible to social and economic progress for blacks, women, Hispanics and other minorities. Given the conservative tenor of the times, all liberal agencies must strive to ensure that the implementation of these laws is maintained. The federal government must not be permitted to shirk its role as a guarantor of social justice for all.

*A national commitment to the advancement of democracy and human rights around the world. Our world is an increasingly interdependent one, particularly in an economic sense. American goods are competing with products made in authoritarian and totalitarian regimes which exploit workers, trammel independent trade unions and thereby undercut American workers. The AFL-CIO has taken an important lead in attempting to remedy the situation by offering assistance to trade unions in the Third World through its international agencies. While we realize that many emerging countries, depleted of hard-currency reserves, must manage by making and selling products using their most abundant resource, cheap labor, the government has a responsibility to assist workers in this country affected by the importation of these products and the relocation of American companies overseas.

* * *

Clearly, such an agenda is not and cannot be specifically black. Continuing black economic progress and equal opportunity are not contingent on the government providing "special treatment" to blacks. Any preferential approach postulated along racial, ethnic, religious or sexual lines will only, in the long run, disrupt a multicultural society. However, special privileges can be provided to those who have been exploited or denied opportunities in a multicultural society, if that special treatment is predicated along class lines, precisely because all groups have a depressed class that would benefit. Therefore, an agenda that is class-oriented can unite a potent coalition of blacks and whites, Christians and Jews, workers and the poor that can, through political action, restore the concept of equal opportunity.

The issues raised in such an agenda are a matter of concern for white blue collar workers, for recent college graduates anxious about a stagnant job market, for young professional couples slowly realizing that they cannot seem to reach the same prosperity that their parents did twenty years ago on three times the salary their parents made. Such an agenda, if implemented, would do much to provide to all groups the opportunity for social and economic progress. It would support equal access to avenues of advancement; it would enlarge the area of freedom for all Americans.

America's Alliances & The Imperial Conflict

Zbigniew Brzezinski

America owes the flexibility of its alliances and friendships to external and internal influences. Externally there was the defensive reaction that shaped the initial American security ties with Western Europe and the Far East after World War II, and the generous economic recovery plans for the war-devastated protectorates that soon followed. Internally there was the multiethnic character of U.S. society itself. In contrast to the Soviet Union, where multiethnicity is subordinated to the predominant nation and could eventually prompt a dangerous internal implosion, American multiethnicity has produced a reverse cultural "explosion," influencing the countries from which many Americans originated.

It reaches beyond the obvious ties with Great Britain. The deep-seated popularity of America in many countries, such as Italy, Ireland and Poland, is derived directly from the impact on their populations of the many millions of

America's Alliances

relatives who have become Americans. It reinforces the positive, attractive appeal of the American way of life and creates political sympathies that further cement the formal relationships. It also permits the United States more deliberately to exploit this advantage through the deployment in foreign service or business positions of Americans with particular foreign affinities. As the number of Asian-Americans grows, the same process is beginning to be repeated in relation to Korea, Japan, China, India and Southeast Asia.

Finally, political ties of America's imperial system of alliances are reinforced by the dynamic and highly creative character of socioeconomic change in America. It provides a model for political and economic development, and it prompts the voluntary flow to America of hundreds of thousands of foreign students. All of this spins a web of relationships at least as important as the initial extension abroad of American military power.

As a result of these factors--but particularly of the transoceanic character of U.S. power--America's dependencies do tend to view themselves as genuine allies, and in fact they are such allies. This is not to ignore the reality of political differences and economic conflicts with the United States, but such dissension occurs within a framework of predominantly shared interests, with geographical distance creating political attraction. (The neighbor of my neighbor is my friend but not my neighbor!)

In contrast, the contiguous territorial character of the Soviet empire means that Moscow is seen by its neighbors as inherently threatening and dominating. Hence, even its formal allies are in many respects resentful and potentially unreliable. Communist China and Yugoslavia, both geographically proximate to the Soviet Union, broke with the Kremlin. The split with Yugoslavia set a dangerous precedent for Eastern Europe, and the rupture with China was especially damaging to the Soviet quest for continental predominance. Not surprisingly, Moscow's most genuine friends have been such geographically distant countries as Cuba and Vietnam.

* * *

The imperial conflict between Washington and Moscow highlights basic differences of attitude and practice toward wider international arrangments. The multiethnic character of America focuses particular attention on the issue of national self-determination. Today, that issue is of particular relevance in the conflict in Afghanistan and over the East-West division of Europe.

The United States must continue to keep alive the issue of the Soviet occupation of Afghanistan. This requires a three-pronged strategy. *First*, the fighting: the United States must keep supplying the Afghan resistance with money, weapons and ammunition. It must upgrade the equipment provided to the *mujahedeen*, including delivering more advance weaponry such as heat-seeking antiaircraft missiles.

Second, world opinion: the United States should assist more direct mass media coverage of the war itself by improving arrangements for television and radio coverage. This will help to intensify international condemnation of Moscow--the highest cost the Soviet Union is paying for its aggression. Soviet standing has already declined significantly in the Third World, particularly among Muslim countries. India, too, should be encouraged to change its attitude of benign acceptance of Soviet aggression and brutality. If New Delhi were to become more critical of Moscow, the Soviet calculus of costs and benefits might shift toward

America's Alliances

finding a way out. The United States should emphasize to the Indians that India can promote better U.S.-Soviet relations only by contributing to a peaceful solution of the Soviet-Afghan war--and that this will become possible only when Moscow concludes that the political costs of the venture are prohibitively high.

Third, diplomacy: the United States must prepare a diplomatic formula for the disengagement of Soviet forces. As well as the *mujahedeen* have fought, they can never expect to defeat the Soviet Union militarily. At the same time, the Soviets will not disengage voluntarily unless a way can be found to ensure that a Soviet withdrawal does not make Afghanistan an anti-Soviet outpost. To reassure Moscow, the United States should make clear that it would be prepared to participate along with the Soviet Union, China, Pakistan and India in a five-power agreement to guarantee the genuine neutrality of Afghanistan. This might be modeled on the Austrian Peace Treaty of 1955. In addition, the United States could propose that the prompt removal of Soviet forces from Afghanistan be accompanied by the temporary introduction of peacekeeping forces from Islamic countries with foreign policies not unfriendly to the Soviet Union, such as Algeria or Syria. This might reassure Moscow that the departure of the Soviet troops would not be followed by the massacre of all pro-Soviet Afghans.

In short, the goal for a political solution should be external neutralization and internal self-determination. Over time, the combination of mounting international condemnation and increasingly effective *mujahedeen* resistance might persuade the Kremlin to accept this formula. The Kremlin might calculate that its longer-range hopes regarding internal unrest in Iran and Pakistan are better served by a breathing spell that helps to cool anti-Soviet passions among the Muslims.

Perhaps the best deterrent to a continued Soviet push southward exists within the Soviet Union itself--and it represents an opportunity that the United States has so far failed to exploit. Muslims in the Soviet Union now number approximately 55 million people, and they have been subdued--or "Sovietized"--on the surface. It should be recalled, however, that local resistance to Soviet--or, in reality, Great Russian--domination took more than a decade of fighting to suppress, ending only in the ealry 1930s. Today, there is considerable evidence of persistent local resentment of Moscow's policy of Russification. Moreover, since Islam has not been extirpated, Soviet Muslims have doubtless been affected by the worldwide resurgence of Islamic culture and religion. There is here the potential for a serious religious-ethnic challenge over Moscow's control of Soviet central Asia.

The "holy war" against the Soviets in Afghanistan, the fundamentalist revolution in Iran, the strong support for the Afghan *mujahedeen*, and the institution of Islamic law in Pakistan, all reflect a similar phenomenon--a widespread awakening of a more self-assertive orientation based on ethnicity and Islamic faith. This new outlook has now collided with Soviet expansionism. At first, Soviet Muslims reacted to the collision with ambivalence, but resentment is developing. The United States can accelerate this alliance of hostility with greatly intensified radio broadcasts beamed at Soviet central Asia. Washington already plans to set up one new broadcasting facility, Radio Free Afghanistan. It should be used to this end, with special programs targeting Soviet Muslims and stressing the anti-Islamic character of Soviet policies in Afghanistan. In addition, the United States should offer technical support for similar efforts from other Islamic countries. The Kremlin leaders are more likely to exercise restraint if they become convinced that regional unrest will inevitably spill over into the Soviet Union itself.

A repressive empire tends to be an expansive empire. Ultimately, a more stable U.S.-Soviet relationship demands a change in both the scope and character of Soviet power. That can take place peacefully; but promoting it is the needed offensive component of a U.S. strategy designed to mitigate American-Soviet hostility and eventually to bring about a more cooperative relationship. But until then, promoting change within the Soviet realm serves--to put it bluntly--as a means for peacefully seizing the geopolitical initiative in the protracted historical conflict.

The suppressed aspiration of East European nations and the internal national contradictions of the modern-day Great Russian empire provide the springboard for seeking two central and interdependent goals. The first is to weaken the Kremlin's offensive capacity by increasing its domestic preoccupations. The second is to promote the pluralization of the Soviet bloc and eventually of the Soviet Union itself by cautiously encouraging national self-assertiveness.

In an interview in 1983, Milovan Djilas made an apt comparison between the Soviet system of national domination and that of the late Ottoman Empire. He noted that both systems fused political and religious or ideological authority at the highest level of the state and that in both cases expansionism was inherent in the system of power itself. The Ottoman Empire, he continued, sought security and confidence through expansion and "even when it started to decay, [it] could not cease to expand...when that expansion was stopped, then the empire started to disintegrate slowly, as national and social rebellions erupted." Drawing a parallel with far-reaching consequences, Djilas concluded: "In the long run, the Soviet Union must disintegrate, and will disintegrate faster if [its] expansionism is stopped."

Stopping that expansionism--especially on the three central Eurasian fronts--can be facilitated by the promotion of internal change within the Soviet realm. A progressively more independent Eastern Europe would certainly reduce the Soviet military threat to Western Europe. A more assertive attitude on the part of the Soviet Muslims, as well as the Ukranians, Balts and other national minorities, would distract the Kremlin. It would increase the Soviet stake in a more accommodating relationship with its neighbors and with the United States.

Eastern Europe is the natural focus for a dilution of Moscow's imperial power. The basic policy formula, advanced a quarter of a century ago in *Foreign Affairs* by William Griffith and this writer, remains generally valid: "...the United States should adopt a policy of what might be called peaceful engagement in Eastern Europe. This policy should: (1) aim at stimulating further diversity in the Communist bloc; (2) thus increasing the likelihood that the East European states can achieve a greater measure of political independence from Soviet domination; (3) thereby ultimately leading to the creation of a neutral belt of states which...would enjoy genuine popular freedom of choice in internal policy while not being hostile to the Soviet Union and not belonging to Western military alliances...." It is important to stress that the goal should not be to transform Eastern Europe into an extension of NATO. The United States should build on the temper in Eastern Europe for self-emancipation. It should seek to create a situation that, in effect, would be the mirror image of the Soviet Union's ambitions in the West: to transform the essence of Eastern Europe's relationship with Moscow without necessarily disrupting its formal framework.

Conditions in Eastern Europe are ripe. Moscow's growing internal socioeconomic difficulties, the evident

America's Alliances

political restlessness in Poland, and the prospects for a significant political and economic crisis in Romania all pose a painful dilemma for the Kremlin. Controlling the Soviet empire means stabilizing Eastern Europe, but stabilizing Eastern Europe means sharing more Soviet economic resources and opening more political safety valves. Judging by Gorbachev's initial moves in Eastern Europe, Moscow is moving in the opposite direction. The Soviets have decreased economic aid and increased pressures for greater economic and political integration of Eastern Europe with the Soviet Union. Even the Communist elites of Eastern Europe do not find this policy congenial.

In these circumstances, the EEC, with the U.S. backing, should offer Eastern Europe economic options that even the Communist regimes (not to speak of the peoples themselves) will find attractive. Enhancement of all-European economic cooperation would lead indirectly to closer political ties, but without the upheaval that would precipitate a direct Soviet response.

* * *

To promote the reemergence of a more genuinely autonomous Eastern Europe, the existence of an independent-minded and increasingly self-assertive Eastern European public opinion is essential. The most important, and perhaps least recognized, service that America has rendered over the years to the preservation of a European identity in Eastern Europe has been its sponsorship since 1950 of Radio Free Europe. These broadcasts, beamed in national languages to the peoples of Eastern Europe, have focused their programming specifically on these countries' internal dilemmas. Though fiercely denounced by the Communist regimes, and though its broadcasts have been frequently jammed,

RFE has almost single-handedly prevented Moscow from accomplishing a central objective: the isolation of Eastern Europe from the rest of Europe and the ideological indoctrination of its peoples. Today, according to the systematic polling undertaken among East European travelers to Western Europe (which because of selective passport policies tends to bias the sample toward those least opposed to the Communist regimes), RFE audiences in Eastern Europe include 66 percent of the adult population in Poland, 63 percent in Romania, 59 percent in Hungary, 40 percent in Bulgaria and 38 percent in Czechoslovakia. In addition, the fact that the East European publics have this alternative source of news forces the Communist mass media not only to be more informative but to respond to criticisms raised in the RFE broadcasts.

With the onset of new communications techniques, such as videocassettes, miniaturized printers and word processors, the opportunities have widened for a more massive intellectual and cultural offensive. Totalitarian control over mass communications is now easier to pierce, and the audiences will grow ever more receptive as East Europeans chafe at Moscow's cultural and economic backwardness, which is denying them the fruits of today's material and technological revolution. As that resentment intensifies, the attraction of a more cooperative relationship with Western Europe will grow. Even the Communist rulers of Eastern Europe--many of whom are more motivated by the desire to stay in power than by the goal of propagating communism--will be susceptible to this pull from the West.

It is worth reiterating that the appeal of freedom and plenty should be the principal focus of the West's peaceful engagement in Eastern Europe. Moscow will not accept political changes that reduce its power. But history teaches that Moscow will accommodate itself to gradual changes that it feels are too costly to prevent. Soviet economic and ideological sterility provide powerful impulses for a progressive process in Eastern Europe. The political realities can be transformed even without formal political changes.

As economic cooperation widens and as Communist ideology wanes, it should become possible for the West to negotiate the security issue in central Europe, capitalizing on the East European pressures for the eventual withdrawal of Soviet forces. For example, besides showing more flexibility in the MBFR talks in Vienna, the West should in general put more emphasis on the importance of mutual reductions in conventional forces. At a more distant stage, it might be appropriate to explore the possibility of some forms of denuclearization in specific regions of Europe, possibly in the Balkans, or in Scandinavia (including in such a case the Baltic republics and the Kola Peninsula). Also, NATO might declare that in the event of war those East European states that declare neutrality would be spared Western military retaliation. Although such a proposal would be attacked by the Communist regimes, it would certainly attract the East European publics.

Poland is bound to play a critical but sensitive role in this process. Since Poland is the linchpin state of Soviet control over Eastern Europe, change in Poland is bound to be of vital concern to Moscow. Kremlin leaders want a compliant, stable and preferably weak Poland. A politically fragmented, economically laggard, socially demoralized Poland is less likely to challenge Russian control--and that is a formula that Moscow has applied to Poland since the partitions of the late eighteenth century. But today's Poland is nationally and religiously more homogeneous than ever before because of the loss or extinction of its national minorities. As a result, Moscow faces a dilemma; its efforts to dominate by the time-tested ploy of *divide et impera* might spark an uncontrollable rebellion born out of national frustration and desperation. That rebellion Moscow could certainly crush, but at a prohibitively high cost.

As a result, despite Moscow's apprehensions and martial law, Poland has succeeded in carving out for itself a margin of autonomy that preserves its distinctive national and religious character. That, in turn, tends to foster even more widespread social self-assertion. A quasi-independent society has developed, and pressures have grown for further change in the character of the regime and its relations with the Soviet Union. Most Poles, however, recognize that such a change must come gradually and must not aim for a rupture with the Soviet Union. Gradual and peaceful change could eventually shape a more equitable relationship between Poland and the Soviet Union. This would enhance East European autonomy and reassure Moscow that Poland and Eastern Europe are not being seduced into the camp of the adversary.

It follows from this that Polish membership in the International Monetary Fund and the eventual reinstatement of American Most Favored Nation trading status are geopolitically desirable. Also, U.S. economic sanctions against Poland should be matched by greater U.S. willingness to participate in a Western economic reconstruction package on the condition that the regime engages in genuine reconciliation with its people and the Solidarity leadership. Specific tactical considerations in the timing of a more constructive U.S. initiative--such as waiting for the termination of political repression against the leaders of Solidarity and the promotion of a more genuine dialogue between the regime and society--do not negate the longer-term desirability of fostering all-European economic cooperation. It should be kept in mind that the ultimate victim of such cooperation is bound to be the expansionist Soviet imperial impulse that seeks to isolate Eastern Europe. It would be a historic irony, indeed, if eventually, through such evolutionary change, the Warsaw Pact became less an instrument of Soviet control and more one of regional restraint on Soviet conduct.

* * *

But for such evolutionary change to be truly decisive in altering the intensity and even perhaps the nature of the U.S.-Soviet contest, it has to spill over into the Soviet Union itself. That spillover initially is bound to be quite limited, given the regimented political traditions of the Great Russian empire. But precisely because it is an empire, it cannot be hermetically sealed off through reliance on a self-contained and homogeneous culture as was done in China. The multinational character of the Soviet Union creates fissures and openings, and the inescapable fact is that in the age of both nationalism and a reviving religious fervor the 55 million Soviet Muslims, the 50 million Ukrainians, the 10 million Balts and the other non-Russian nations do not share totally the instinctive and deeply rooted political impulses of the Great Russians.

The United States should give sharper political definition to these trends through greatly intensified use of modern means of communication. The techniques that have proven so effective in breaking down Eastern Europe's isolation should be more actively applied to the Soviet Union itself. The object of the effort should not be to stoke national hatreds or even to foster the disintegration of the Soviet Union. The real opportunity is to mobilize the forces for genuine political participation, for greater national co-determination, for the dispersal of central power and for the termination of heavy-handed central domination that breeds the expansionist impulse. By encouraging the non-Russians to demand greater respect for their national rights, the political process within the Soviet Union can gradually be refocused on a complicated and absorbing question that involves the very essence of a modern political system: the redistribution of political power. Surely from the standpoint of the West, it is more desirable that this issue should become the central concern of the Soviet leadership, and not one of the economic reforms that might enhance the Soviet capacity to compete with the United States.

Today, modern communication techniques make possible a campaign far more ambitious and diversified than the one launched when the United States began to broadcast to the East Europeans on Radio Free Europe and to address the Soviet peoples on Radio Liberty. In recent years, moreover, the Soviet Union has been placed on the ideological defensive. In Western Europe, Communist parties are on the decline. In the Far East, Soviet ideology is irrelevant. Even in Latin America, Moscow's appeal is declining. In the Middle East, the revival of Islamic faith has prevented the Soviets from capitalizing on increased anti-Americanism. Only in southern Africa do conditions favor increased Soviet ideological appeal. In these circumstances, the moment is ripe to take the initiative by an intensified program of multilanguage radio broadcasts, an increased distribution of audiovisual cassettes, and an effort to provide technical support for independent domestic political literature. U.S. funding of such programs should be at least tripled, for expenditures that change Soviet political attitudes are certainly more cost-effective than the arms race. This increase would only cost as much as a few B-1 bombers.

The Soviet Union's socioeconomic stagnation and its multinational makeup create fertile ground for encouraging a more critical political outlook among the Soviet peoples.

America's Alliances

Given decades of doctrinal conditioning and political isolation, the initial receptivity to this effort will be much lower than with the East Europeans. But the national and religious feelings of the non-Russians and the domestic failings of the Communist system do make the Soviet peoples potentially susceptible to aspirations already more widespread in Eastern Europe. When that potential begins to manifest itself, even Milovan Djilas's bold predictions might seem less than startling.

Academic Freedom: Problems and Prospects

Sidney Hook

In this day very few persons will openly declare that they are opposed to academic freedom. The battle for academic freedom was successfully waged over forty years ago. But, just as it would be hazardous to predict the specific beliefs of those who profess "democracy," particularly when prefaced with adjectives like "higher" or "directed" or simply "new" or "people's," it would be difficult to assert that "academic freedom" means the same thing to all who claim to support it. Nonetheless, if we are careful, and are prepared to make relevant distinctions, I believe it is possible to clarify what academic freedom has meant in the history of higher education in the Western world, and particularly in the history of American higher education. Before we declare that academic freedom is present or absent or discuss its problem, we must begin with a working definition.

I offer the following: Academic freedom is the

Academic Freedom

freedom of professionally qualified persons to inquire or investigate, to discuss, publish or teach the truth as they see it in the discipline of their competence, subject to no religious or political control or authority, except the control of standards of professional ethics or the authority of the rational methods by which truths and conclusions are established in the disciplines involved.

This definition is substantially the one elaborated in greater detail by Arthur O. Lovejoy who together with John Dewey founded the American Association of University Professors, the latter as president and the former as secretary. At the time, 1915, academic freedom, as they defined it, could hardly be said to be recognized by most governing boards of American colleges and universities. Even in the 30s, when I served as a member of the Council of the AAUP, its principles were far from being universally accepted. Today, there is hardly a college or university in the country that does not proclaim its allegiance to those principles. Indeed the proclamation and acceptance of these principles have become commonplace. And like other commonplaces, some of its implications are overlooked.

* * *

I want to begin by exploring some of its implications. *First*, it is important to note that academic freedom is defined here not as the freedom to teach the truth but as the freedom *to seek* the truth. What is the difference? Isn't the truth important? Of course it is, but just as important is recognition of the fact that even if one believes in absolute truth, human recognition of the truth, however it be defined, varies; that many things once believed true are no longer accepted by competent inquirers as true; and some things once considered false, like the heliocentric hypothesis, are now considered true. That is why we cannot accept without qualification the Augustinian dictum that error has no rights.

Second, academic freedom is a special right; it is not, despite much rhetoric to the contrary, a human right, or a civil right or a constitutional right. It is the right of the professionally qualified teacher or researcher. What, one may ask, is the difference between a special right like academic freedom and these other rights--human, civil or constitutional? To give a short answer--academic freedom is a right that must be *earned*. All these other rights we enjoy as members of the democratic community. They are our birthright as citizens; they do not have to be earned, and the community has an obligation to prevent others from denying or abridging them. The community and its law-enforcing agencies in a democracy cannot arrogate to themselves, except under carefully defined conditions, the power to limit the exercise of our human and constitutional rights. Freedom of speech gives anyone freedom to talk nonsense anytime, anywhere, barring for the moment laws about public nuisance. But it does not give anyone the right to talk or teach nonsense in a university. One must, so to speak, be professionally qualified to talk nonsense in a university.

Of course, what may appear as nonsense to you, or to the inexpert, may turn out to be the latest in higher wisdom or knowledge. The truths of non-Euclidian geometry, or the view that the simultaneity of two distant events is not absolute but relative to different frames of reference, or current notions in cosmology, quantum physics or genetic engineering, all appeared nonsensical to some when they were first enunciated.

Similarly, one can, under the First Amendment, teach on the street or in one's home anyone who wants to be instructed. But one must be qualified to teach or engage in research before he or she can be permitted to teach in a

Academic Freedom

university classroom or experiment in a laboratory. There are many problems connected with qualification, but we can't dispense with the principle of qualification without making a shambles of our educational system. The whole structure of our social life depends on the recognition of the indispensibility of qualification as a necessary condition of professional performance. Every time we enter a hospital or clinic or entrust ourselves to a public conveyance, we stake our life on the assumption that some adequate tests of qualification have been conducted. And although going to a university is not very risky, no one who values his time or money would enter its classrooms unless he or she assumed that the teachers were qualified to teach their subject.

In this connection a certain feature of qualification must be mentioned which, although not unique to university life, is often misunderstood and productive of needless controversy. No institution, and certainly not a university, can function well if appointment to its staff conveys instant and permanent tenure. In the nature of the case there must be a probation period of varying length before full qualification can be established. When academic freedom is recognized, it holds for the probation period, too. The criteria that must be met before tenure is granted varies with different types of teaching. In those institutions where the greatest stress is placed on excellence of teaching, the criteria will be different from those in which excellence in research and quality of publication are given precedence. I shall not pursue this complex question here. Normally I have found that those who receive an appointment assume that they are entitled to life long or permanent tenure if they conscientiously perform their duties. They are apt to be extremely suspicious of the grounds offered for their nonrenewal after the probation period.

It is at this point that many cases allegedly involving

breaches of academic freedom arise. For the grant of permanent tenure not only completes the rites of passage to full academic citizenship, it confers a lien on the university's future resources of almost three quarters of a million dollars. No responsible faculty or administration can permit the grant of tenure to be taken as a matter of course. Every decision must be considered a major serious educational decision.

A *third* remarkable implication of academic freedom is that if one subscribes to it, one is committed to the belief that the professionally qualified person in pursuit of the truth, and abiding by the canons of professional ethics, has a right to reach any conclusions that seem to him valid. This means he has what I have called the right to heresy in the field of his competence. This is a very momentous inference, for to those who disagree with him it means the right in good faith to be wrong. It means that an honest inquirer will be defended not only when he reaches a heresy that we agree with but a heresy with which we disagree. That is easily said, but experience shows that often it depends on whose ox is being gored. In disciplines where controversy is rife, especially the social sciences and the humanities, this means that where academic freedom exists it will protect the right of a qualified teacher to reach conclusions that some will regard as Communist or fascist or racist or irreligious or un-American.

There is a *fourth* implication of academic freedom that is even more remarkable. I, as a professor, can share a public platform with my grocer, my butcher, my doctor and my lawyer. We all exercise our constitutional right of freedom of speech to advocate the same unpopular or heretical proposal. Select your own particular abomination as an illustration. Let us say voluntary euthanasia or the deportation of illegal aliens or curtailing social security. Every one of my fellow speakers may pay a very large price

Academic Freedom

for the expression of his opinions. They may lose trade, or patients or clients to a point where their very livelihood may be affected. I, however, to the extent that I have academic freedom claim and enjoy complete immunity from any institutional sanctions. Neither my salary nor my prospects of promotion can be affected. In a sense I am experiencing a privilege or freedom that comparatively few of my fellow citizens have. I am absolved of the normal costs of unpopularity and sometimes even of my defiance of convention. Coupled with the fact that once I acquire tenure, I cannot be deprived of it except by a long and arduous due process--rarely invoked in universities--this reinforces the exceptional nature of my vocational rights as contrasted with most other vocations and professions.

* * *

It is necessary to stand off and examine in perspective the remarkable character of the right to academic freedom. It is remarkable in that, as distinct from what existed in any other period of human history, it involves not only the tolerance of intellectual heresy but its legal support. It is remarkable in that it offers safeguards in ways that are unprecedented, against the price or costs of intellectual heresies, and in that it has upheld the right of teachers to exercise their responsibilities of citizenship on the same terms as their neighbors without suffering academic sanctions. And it is remarkable, above all, because of its uniqueness in the long history of civilization, in its limited jurisdiction to certain areas of the Western and American world, and in the recency of its emergence in those areas.

There was no academic freedom in the ancient world, not even in democratic Athens, as the death of Socrates attests. There was no academic freedom during the medieval synthesis, the Renaissance, the Reformation or the Enlightenment. There was no academic freedom in colonial or revolutionary America or in England, where instruction was largely in the hands of the clergy. Academic freedom was an un-American importation from Imperial Germany where it first took root in the University of Berlin in 1810 at a time, interestingly enough, when there was less political democracy in Prussia and the rest of Germany than in the United States or Great Britain. When I began teaching in the American university in 1927, academic freedom and faculty governance were in a very rudimentary state. Contracts were for one year with no legal presumption of renewal. The status of the faculty was little better than that of hired men in industry except that one's private life and public activity could more readily affect one's academic future than in other pursuits. Boards of Trustees often intervened directly into educational affairs. Gradually things improved, especially as members of the AAUP made their way up the administrative ladder. The turning point was the adoption of the AAUP's Basic Statement of Principles not only by the Association of American Colleges and Universities but by forty-seven national professional organizations of scholars and teachers embracing almost the entire spectrum of the arts and sciences. By the end of the Second World War, the battle for academic freedom was essentially won, although several problems on procedural matters remained to be clarified.

The very recency and rarity of academic freedom give rise to the question: why should the community that either directly or indirectly through tax exemption underwrites the great costs of university education support the institution of academic freedom? There are many reasons but we can sum them all up in the statement: because it believes that it is to its own ultimate interest to do so. It believes that the discovery of new truths and the extension of the frontiers of

Academic Freedom

knowledge are more effectively furthered by the presence of academic freedom than by its absence. It believes that fidelity to the mission of the university will result in the accumulation of bodies of reliable objective knowledge that may be used as guides or tests of policy by legislators and citizens. It gives relative autonomy to the university not for the pleasure and enjoyment of its teachers and researchers but for the good of society.

* * *

But it should be obvious that this precious right to academic freedom carries with it certain duties and responsibilities about which we unfortunately hear less and less. It is certainly true that academic freedom protects the expression of heresy, but that does not mean that "anything goes" in the way of classroom or research behavior, that one is free to do or not do *anything* he or she pleases to do. The grant of academic freedom is based on the assumption that the mission of the universities is to search for the truth, and therefore on the assumption that the professor or researcher is truly *seeking* to reach the truth or the best warranted conclusion on the available evidence. The assumption is that he or she is a free agent, not under orders from an outside group to indoctrinate or to cook his evidence, not bought, not a fanatic committed in advance of inquiry to a predetermined conclusion regardless of the evidence. In short, the assumption behind the grant of academic freedom is that the professor is a scholar, not a propagandist, and this is the source of the duties and responsibilities correlative to the exercise of his freedom.

It is noteworthy but rarely acknowledged that the 1940 Basic Statement on Academic Freedom of the AAUP explicitly asserts that academic freedom "carries with it duties correlative with rights." It enumerates quite a few, e.g.: "The teacher is entitled to freedom in the classroom in discussing his subject but he should be careful not to introduce into his teaching controversial matter which has no relation to his subject." (It seems to me that even if the matter is noncontroversial but has no relation to the subject, it does not belong in the classroom.) The duties enumerated in the AAUP statement are not confined to the teacher's behavior in the classroom. It reminds him that "as a man of learning and an education officer, he should remember that the public may judge his profession and his institution by his utterances. Hence he should at all times be accurate, should exercise appropriate restraint, should show respect for the opinions of others, and should make every effort to indicate that he is not an institutional spokesman." In a further statement in 1956, the AAUP adds:

> The academic community has a duty to defend society and itself from subversion of the educational process by dishonest tactics, including political conspiracies to deceive students and lead them into acceptance of dogmas or false causes. Any member of the academic profession who has given reasonable evidence that he uses such tactics should be proceeded against forthwith, and should be expelled from his position if his guilt is established by rational procedure.

Similar sentiments are expressed in the famous declaration of the Graduate School of the New School for Social Research established by exiles from totalitarian countries.

> The New School knows that no man can teach well, nor should he be permitted to teach at all, unless he is prepared "to follow the truth of scholarship wherever it may lead." No inquiry is ever made as to whether a lecturer's private views are conservative, liberal, or radical; orthodox or agnostic;

views of the aristocrat or commoner. Jealously safeguarding this precious principle, the New School stoutly affirms that a member of any political party or group which asserts the right to dictate in matters of science or scientific opinion is not free to teach the truth and thereby is disqualified as a teacher.

Equally the New School holds that discrimination on grounds of race, religion or country of origin either among teachers or students runs counter to every profession of freedom and has no place in American education.

It follows from the foregoing that the faculty that extends its *protection* to its members who exercise their right to academic freedom must also be prepared to *discipline* those who violate the duties and responsibilities of academic freedom. There is no necessity for state legislatures or Congress to investigate where questions of professional ethics are involved. Rather, academic bodies are the best qualified to determine the fitness of their colleagues to teach and to give the benefit of due process to those charged with unfitness or violation of professional trust. It stands to reason that the unwillingness of a faculty to administer its own standards of objective scholarship and intellectual integrity, its indifference to what is taught and how it is taught, or to whether anything at all is taught in its classes is both wrong and foolish. It will not only degrade the quality of the degrees it bestows and affect its scholarly standing, but sooner or later it will provoke community alarm and interference. In public institutions whose budget is underwritten by tax money, it is safe to predict that any academic scandal that seems to indicate laxity in the application of proper scholarly standards is sure to give rise to legislative investigation.

Faculties should be very jealous of their scholarly reputations on teaching and research. Self-appraisal and self-criticism of their curricular offering should be an on-going process. The enforcement of the statement about the responsibilities and duties of scholarship should not be treated as pious platitudes. They should be as vigorously enforced as the principles of academic freedom are defended. When that is done, faculties can be prepared to stand up to any relevant legislative inquiry. They can with eloquent dignity point out that the legislature has the legal power to establish or not establish any educational institution, whether liberal or professional. But once that decision is made, then it is within the professional competence of the educators to operate and control that institution without let or hindrance from those not professionally qualified, including the legislators. For that is the meaning of academic freedom. And if the university faculties have lived up to their academic mission, they will ultimately win community support.

* * *

Can the ideals of academic freedom be sustained? Today those ideals are not so much endangered by the traditional enemies of academic freedom, the church and state, but by forces within the university itself.

I have referred to the mission of the university as providing the context of academic freedom. I have defined that mission in terms of the pursuit of intellectual ends-- discovery, clarification, criticism aimed at reaching the various modes of truth. But during the last decades there has emerged in some quarters a new conception of the university that discards the traditional objective of scholarship and regards the university as primarily an agency of social change to effect political goals. This view is not satisfied to present programs to the democratic electorate for acceptance or rejection but insists on the right to use the classrooms for political purposes. In the past the classroom and univer-

Academic Freedom

sity have often been used for such political and religious purposes, but according to the conception of academic freedom I have defended this has been a lapse from the mission of the university and the ideal of objectivity. But the new view challenges the very conception of objective truth as a superstition. In effect it regards the university as an arena of struggle for conflicting political views, and refuses to recognize any distinction between the quest for objective truth and propaganda. It accepts whatever freedom it can acquire but refuses to recognize any responsibilities and duties. It proudly carries the bias and partisanship of the hustings and marketplace into the university, which then becomes transformed into a battlefield of warring groups struggling for domination.

Here is a typical statement by a representative of this point of view:

> The social university is not primarily concerned with the abstract pursuit of scholarship, but with the utilization of knowledge obtained thru scholarship to obtain social change. Therefore it does not recognize the right of its members to do anything they wish under the name of academic freedom; instead it assumes that all its members are committed to social change. To give an example, a course in riot control would simply be declared out of place in such a university, while a course in methods of rioting might be perfectly appropriate. (Alan Wolfe, "The Myth of a Free Scholar" *The Center Magazine*, July 1969.)

There are even more extreme statements of this position. If such a view of the university prevailed or even achieved wide currency, I doubt whether any community would support its existence for long. In my view of academic freedom any qualified teacher has the freedom to say or write or advocated such a view of the university, but if he were to *act* on it and subordinate his teaching and research not to the controls of scholarship and evidence, he would be in violation of the duties and responsibilities of academic freedom. He or she should be held to account by faculty peers. And if these peers lacked the courage to do so, both their institutions and the cause of academic freedom would suffer irreparable damage.

Unfortunately the politicization of many American universities since the 60s and the introduction of some new disciplines in which the expression of only one point of view is tolerated have created a climate of opinion on some campuses very hostile to the principles of academic freedom as I have defined them. The situation is exacerbated by the intolerance of radical extremists among student bodies who refuse to permit the expression of views with which they are unsympathetic. It would hardly be an exaggeration to say that since the so-called Free Speech Movement at Berkeley there is no longer freedom of speech, even for invited scholars, to present and uphold publicly the views of the American government. Contrast the ugly treatment meted out to Jeane Kirkpatrick, the violent disruption of her meetings, with the friendly reception accorded to Communist Angela Davis, a notorious apologist for the Soviet Gulag and other oppressive Communist regimes. Not so long ago the President of Harvard had to plead with the Cambridge academic community to extend the traditional courtesies of a hearing to visiting officials of the American government. These violations of elementary political and civic freedoms continue primarily because faculty is unwilling to discipline disrupters in accordance with principles of due process worked out in collaboration with student bodies of recent years.

Even more widespread, continuous and educationally disastrous is the conversion of many classrooms, particularly in the humanities and social sciences, into political pulpits, sometimes on matters unrelated to the theme of the course and outside the field of competence of the instructor. Almost always the bias of the teaching and preaching is directed in one way--*against* American policies and institutions, without a scholarly, fair or balanced presentation of the issues. Horror stories about such excesses abound. One English instructor, whose area of specialization has nothing at all to do with political or foreign affairs, teaches his class that there is currently more injustice in America than there was in Nazi Germany. Another, a history instructor, converts his class into guerrilla theatre to attack American policy in Nicaragua. A professor holding a joint appointment in psychology and anthropology teaches that there are three varieties of racism of which Zionism is one. Still another professor alleges that the holocaust of the Jewish population in Europe is a Zionist myth.

* * *

How can such violations of the ethics of teaching and scientific inquiry be combatted without opening the door to other and possibly worse evils? I repeat, certainly not by legislative investigation or action on a state or national level. This threatens the relative autonomy of the university and the whole conception of academic freedom which has developed to serve us well in this country only in our century.

Nor can these violations be combatted properly by a proposal recently presented by a group called Accuracy in Academia. This proposal calls for the organization of concerned students and others on campuses to monitor the classrooms of teachers. Through the use of tapes and notes they plan to record the statements of teachers that they deem seriously in error and send them to a central source where they will be vetted. If the statements are regarded as ill-founded, the professors will be requested to correct them in class, failing which wide publicity will be given to the offending remarks.

Those who have advanced this proposal are unwittingly damaging the cause of academic freedom and are playing into the hands of the very individuals whose excesses have aroused their sense of outrage.

First, most teachers will justifiably resent the assumption that what they say will be monitored and judged by persons who have no professional standing. *Second*, in pursuing and analysing an idea, new or old, it may be necessary to explore critically positions and statements that may be at great variance from accepted views, even if they are ultimately rejected. *Third*, anyone with any academic experience knows how hazardous it is to rely on students' notes to determine what has been said, and in what context. *Fourth*, teachers with heretical views will be discouraged from expressing their judgments lest a hue and cry be raised by some hysterical devotee of orthodoxy, thus depriving both students and the community of insights that challenge accepted doctrine. *Finally*, the grant of academic freedom carries with it a trust in the *bona fides* of the qualified teacher that is challenged in advance by this proposal.

Among the most vehement critics of Accuracy in Academia have been the very persons who are committed to a propagandistic, illiberal and predominantly anti-Western stance in their teaching, and who are shouting that academic freedom is threatened while they themselves continue to violate its duties and responsibilities. Others, who only recently kept a discreet silence when free speech and academic freedom were being denied to Jeane Kirkpatrick, as Jefferson Lecturer, at Berkeley, and at Minnesota and other univerisities, have rushed into the fray with hackles

Academic Freedom

flaring. At Stanford University, one of the leaders of the movement to deprive the Fellows of the Hoover Institution (whose scholarship and recognized achievements are beyond his range) of their academic freedom on the alleged ground of their conservative orientation now paints himself as a target, as a victim. In the hubbub that has been raised by this thoughtless proposal, public attention will be distracted from the actual sapping and undermining of the principles of academic freedom that have accompanied the growing politicization of American universities.

* * *

Where does this leave us? If we reject any legislative oversight and forego such shortsighted and self-defeating proposals as those of Accuracy in Academia, how shall we combat the multiple abuses of the academic ethic?

By exercising our academic freedom *publicly* to criticize its violations on the campuses on which they occur, by insisting that administrations enforce the guarantees of free speech to visiting scholars and other guests, and by initiating disciplinary action against those guilty of disruption. If administrations persist in their policies of self-defeating appeasement and refuse to enforce the provisions of the disciplinary codes established on most campuses by joint student-faculty committees, resort should be made by concerned faculty to the Civil Rights Law.

In the last analysis, the academic health of the university and the integrity of the academic ethic can only be upheld by the faculties themselves. So far it seems that those members of the faculties who seek to subvert the academic mission, who deny that there are objective standards of scholarship, who insist that all teaching is a form of propaganda, seem to show more courage in proclaiming these absurdities and peddling their nostrums than those who disagree with them. On some campuses it may court unpopularity to criticize publicly the mouthings of radical fanatics and the duplicities of ritualistic liberals who deny that there is any danger to intellectual and political freedom from the left. But unpopularity is a small price to pay to recall the university to its mission.

Ultimately we must rest our faith in the intelligence of our students to assess for themselves the truth of conflicting claims. But they must be aware of the existence of conflicting claims; they must hear the other side; they must hear the criticism of the nonsense about the Nazification of American culture by the apologists for Gorbachev, Castro, Ortega and their similars. Our students must be reassured that as a group their teaching faculties do subscribe to a tested body of knowledge painstakingly wrested from ignorance by our forebears; that they do actively participate in the process by which we differentiate between what is probably true from what is demonstrably false; that they are willing to stand up and defend the intellectual and scholarly legacy entrusted to them against politically inspired attacks, regardless of the political spectrum from which such attacks originate. Scholars cannot entrust to others the chores of intellectual hygiene. Upon them rests the responsibility of maintaining academic freedom in a free society.

Freedom, Civil Liberties & the Polls

Burns W. Roper

Do you think a married woman who has no children under sixteen and whose husband makes enough to support her should or should not be allowed to take a job if she wants to? Would you eat in a restaurant that served both Negro and white people? Do you believe that newspapers and magazines should be allowed to print a fine painting of a nude? Do you consider it all right, unfortunate or wicked when young men have sexual relations before marriage? Do you think it is indecent for men to wear topless bathing suits for swimming?

One could not imagine asking questions such as these today. But all of them were, in fact, asked by national polls around the time that Freedom House was formed. The mere existence of questions such as these shows at least one dramatic way in which times have changed over the forty-five years of Freedom House's existence.

In many respects things have not changed, or have

changed in one direction and then turned back toward the other in a pendulum swing. But in one very fundamental way, opinion has changed steadily and hugely over the last forty to fifty years. That change has been in the American public's tolerance--or at least toleration--of minority views, different peoples and "deviant" practices.

Without even knowing what the results to the five preceding questions are, it is clear, merely from the fact that they were asked, that prejudice was extensive and that many Americans obviously held narrow, intolerant views.

* * *

Of all the changes that opinion polls have recorded over the years, easily the most dramatic as well as the most consistent are the changes in toleration. There is far greater tolerance--or toleration--of Blacks, of Italians, of Catholics, of Jews and of most other racial or religious minorities that polls have asked about. The increase in toleration, however is by no means limited to racial or religious groups. It has also occurred in the area of sex--in two respects. There is far less of a double standard than there used to be. Few people today think premarital sex is alright for men but not for women. It is either acceptable for both, or for neither. Additionally, there is increasing acceptance of what used to be sexual taboos. Premarital sex is not frowned upon as it is used to be. People have come to accept, if not endorse, couples living together without benefit of marriage. Acceptance of divorce has increased. Acceptance of nudity has increased.

This is not to say that all whites treat all blacks as they do themselves; that there aren't many who wouldn't prefer that their sons not marry a Catholic or their daughters not marry a Jew. This is not to say that people *endorse* or *advocate* couples living together without being married. Or that people approve of "men's magazines" or X-rated films. But it is to say that people increasingly tolerate such actions, conditions and objects.

Homosexuality, too, is increasingly tolerated, even if not endorsed. One might assume that the burgeoning AIDS epidemic would turn at least some people in an anti-homosexual direction. In fact, a certain amount has been said about AIDS being a demonstration of God's disapproval of homosexuality. A Roper poll question, asked well before AIDS became a public issue, and repeated after AIDS and its homosexual orientation had received widespread notice, showed an *increase* in tolerance for homosexuals rather than a decrease. The question* asked people which of the following two statements best described their views.

	1985	1978	1977
a. "Homosexuals should be guaranteed equal treatment under the law in jobs and housing."	66%	57%	60%
b. "It should be *legal* to keep people out of jobs and housing if they are homosexuals."	22%	28%	28%
c. Don't know	12%	15%	12%

*The question reads as follows: "Some time ago, the citizens of Miami voted to repeal a county ordinance that banned discrimination in employment and housing based on a person's sexual preferences. The ordinance essentially meant that someone who is homosexual could not be kept from holding a particular job or living in any type of housing simply because he or she is homosexual. Which of these two statements best describes how you feel about the law and discrimination against homosexuals?" (Card shown to respondents)

Freedom & the Polls

It was not until the 1980s that there was any significant publicity about or awareness of AIDS. By the summer of 1985, 97 percent of the adult American public had heard about AIDS and it ranked only behind cancer as a disease the American public most feared. Most people were aware that AIDS was particularly prevalent in the homosexual community. Nevertheless, the 1985 results showed people more favorable, rather than less, towards protection of homosexuals under the law.

Clearly, if there is less prejudice today against all kinds of minorities and various types of "deviant" behavior, this means that individual civil liberties are strengthened and that more and more people in this country know greater and greater freedom.

* * *

What else do opinion polls tell us about the American public and freedom? A Roper Poll for the Cable News Network and *U.S. News and World Report* conducted in June 1986 asked people whether each of seven factors was a major reason for the United States' greatness, something of a reason, or not a reason. The factors asked about included such things as: our melting pot culture, our system of free public education, our natural resources, our moral principles and religious beliefs, etc. Rated highest of all as a major reason for this country's greatness was "our freedom and liberty"--by 88 percent of the adult American public. While majorities rated all but one of the factors as a major reason, none of the others came close. The next highest rated factor, seen as a major reason by 72 percent, was "our free enterprise system."

It has often been said that Americans do not appreciate their freedom, that they are inclined to take it for granted and do not recognize what a precious asset it is. These results would seem to indicate that the American public is not only very conscious of the fact that it *has* freedom and liberty, but is fully appreciative of its *importance* in the nation's well-being.

Another question in the same survey tends to underscore this. People were asked which of a half dozen symbols best represents America in their view. The "official" symbol of the United States, the American flag, came in *second* with 46 percent naming it. In clear first place was the Statue of Liberty with 57 percent saying it best represents America. To be sure, these results were obtained during all of the pre-Fourth of July, 100th birthday hype about the rejuvenated statue. Nevertheless, it is significant that the made-in-France statue easily surpassed the American flag. Such things as the Washington Monument, the White House and the Lincoln Memorial were also-rans. In fact, in third place was still another item with the word "liberty" in it-- the Liberty Bell.

It seems clear, both from the trend results of increasing toleration of all manner of things and from current readings on Americans' attitudes towards America, that individual liberties and individual freedoms are strong and have been getting stronger. The trend towards greater toleration has been steady and persistent. It has been without noticeable hesitation and certainly without pendulum swings. At this writing, several events have occurred which suggest that at least hesitation, or possibly even reversal, is beginning to take place.

The Justice Department has issued an opinion that an employer may dismiss an employee who has AIDS if, in the *employer's opinion*, the continued employment of the AIDS victim would be likely to cause the spread of AIDS in the employer's workforce. As the Fourth of July and the re-

Freedom & the Polls

dedication of the Statue of Liberty moved still closer, the Supreme Court handed down a ruling upholding the sodomy laws of the state of Georgia, thus granting the right of the state to look into the bedrooms of consenting homosexuals and, maybe, also paving the way for enforcement of sodomy laws between consenting partners of opposite sexes--even married couples--since the Georgia sodomy law says nothing about gender. Shortly after our Fourth of July recommitment to liberty and freedom, Attorney General Meese's Pornography Commission issued its report calling for less permissive interpretations of the First Amendment in the areas of obscenity and pornography. At about the same time, a group of parents in Hawkins County, Tennessee, brought a legal action against the school system to rid the system of, or at least provide alternatives to, *The Wizard of Oz* and other "un-Christian" teaching aids!

It is conceivable that, after at least a fifty-year march in the direction of greater toleration, we are about to see it reversed. It would certainly be imprudent to say that because the trend toward tolerance has been steady for fifty years, it will continue for another fifty years. It is possible the nation has reached its breaking point in terms of greater and greater personal liberty and personal freedom--at least temporarily. However, my guess would be that these recent signs of encroachment on freedom are temporary blips on the radar screen and that, for the foreseeable future, we will continue, whether at greater or slower speed, in the direction of still more toleration. (I should quickly add that my credentials are far greater in the area of *measuring* public opinion than of *predicting* it.) Future polls will measure the accuracy of this prediction.

To this point, we have examined poll results in a descriptive way. We have observed what polls have told us about the state of liberty and the presence or absence of individual freedoms. But polls can do more than describe the state of liberty and the condition of freedom. They also help achieve greater--or lesser--liberty and freedom. If people are truly fed up with the trend to permissiveness, with "unnatural" sex, with excessive displays of flesh, future polls will reveal that public discontent and a combination of legislation as well as court rulings will undoubtedly start to restrict the liberties and freedoms that currently exist in these areas.

In a democracy, voting is the traditional method by which the public exercises its will and, hence, its individual rights. In two ways polls supplement the citizen's expressions of his or her desires through the vote. The vote itself is a rather crude tool. It can, for example, tell you that people want Reagan instead of Carter but without telling you why. Do they want Reagan in a positive sense, or are they repelled by Carter in a negative sense? If it is the former, what attracts them to Reagan? If it is the latter, why have they had enough to Carter? Polls can serve to complement and explain the simple "yea" or "nay" vote of the citizenry.

In addition to explaining a vote, polls can serve as a continuing referendum--as interim elections--between the formal conventional election-day exercises of the public's will.

Public opinion is a force in any society, even in a rigid authoritarian society, but most particularly it is a force in the United States. One of the main ways in which public opinion is expressed in this country is through opinion polls. In fact, it can be argued that public opinion, as revealed in poll results, has far more influence on both our governmental and business systems than it should. It may come as a surprise to learn that I will not refute that argument. Too often, poll results are presented as the will or conviction of the public when, in fact, the poll results do not reflect public opinion at all, but merely reveal the response of people to the particular wording of a particular question.

Unfortunately, 76 percent looks just as authoritative when it represents the unconsidered response of an uninformed public as when it represents the deep conviction of a very much involved public. The ridiculous error statement that almost invariably accompanies the publication of the poll's results, and that has nothing whatsoever to do with the poll's validity, adds to the credibility of even the most erroneous and misleading polls.*

If opinion polls sometimes have more influence than they deserve, it is equally true that they sometimes have less influence than they merit. It is not uncommon for people to write off poll results because two polls show opposite findings. Polls that show opposite findings are often extremely revealing. Opposite findings can result from genuine public ambivalence. They can also result from widespread ignorance. Either way, the findings are meaningful.

It is to be hoped that consumers of poll data will become more discerning in separating reliable from unreliable polls, for polls potentially represent a great tool for realizing freedom as well as a valid device for assessing it.

---

*Sampling error deals only with the error that may be attributable to interviewing only a small sample of people rather than all of the people-- all of the people, that is, who are willing to be interviewed. It provides no measure of how different the results might be given a major--or even a minor--change in wording. It has nothing to do with whether the survey is presenting informed opinion or top of the head reaction to a stimulus.

The Press vs. Press Responsibility in a Pre-Messianic Age

Leonard R. Sussman

Since movable type first empowered journalists, they have been targets of abuse (and worse), their products often censored or directed by state power. Press freedom, which exists in 24 percent of the countries, is derived from the broader acknowledgement that the individual citizen has certain rights, among them the right to expression and access to information. The free press is a latter-day phenomenon, practiced nowhere more diversely than in the United States this past half-century. Yet, as with all rights, press freedom has limitations, both in law and in ethics. The ideal in a democratic society, therefore, is avoidance of all but the most essential national-security restrictions determined by government, and the equal avoidance of journalistic license which harms the society and undermines the credibility of the press itself. What is sought, then, is a free and responsible press.

Yet for nearly a half-century American journalists have

repeatedly rejected calls for public self-examination of "press responsibility," calls that come from their peers, distinguished U.S. academics, and intergovernmental forums such as the United Nations Educational, Scientific and Cultural Organization (UNESCO). Indeed, the decade-long debates at UNESCO over "press responsibility" have been regarded by U.S. journalists as little more than governmental efforts to license, censor and penalize the press for unpleasant reportage. Some of that defensive response was merited, but discussion of the composition of a free and responsible press is more than ever necessary for free societies above all, and certainly for those that aspire to greater freedom. Actual performance of the news media, at their best, is better than ever; at their worst, more destructive than when communications technologies were less pervasive. Attempts to evade public examination of the role of journalism in this Information Age have not strengthened the free press; they have, rather, added to the public's sense of alienation, and the press's loss of credibility.

My purpose here is to outline the elusive question of press responsibility over the past forty-five years. Covering the daily deformities of a largely imperfect world is the rough-and-ready job of the news media. It is too much to expect journalism to produce the Messianic Age. Yet the performance of the news media, as few other occupations, can influence societies perceptively for better or worse.

* * *

The age into which Freedom House was born in 1941 was murderous, even genocidal. Human freedom, an ideal nurtured by despair, inspired hope of peace-with-freedom on only a distant day. Millions were still to die, many without knowing why. Survivors would learn only vaguely the breadth of that human tragedy, though they could understand the consumate evil that had been defeated.

Their knowledge would be limited by wartime censorship and propaganda and, at war's end, even by the journalistic instinct (there are always notable exceptions) to focus on today's, ever *today's,* story: Leave the past, even the immediate past, to history; and avoid the future before it happens; then for a fleeting moment, the present is news: If not hurriedly recorded and appropriately slotted in one of few categories of "newsworthiness," the event or personality passes into limbo. That journalistic mode favors the exciting, the exotic, the controversial, the criminal. It ignores or underplays the "need to know." This pattern prevails for local and national news, and especially for foreign news-reporting. As a consequence, many Americans have only a parochial understanding of the fundamental interests and aspirations which move the rest of the world.

That pattern has improved somewhat since 1941. Yet in the intervening forty-five years America has assumed leadership of what may still be called the free world, and the modes and channels of communication have multiplied many times over. "The lights are going out all over Europe," reported America's foremost radio journalist as World War II began. After the war ended, in just the next few moments (when clocked against the span of recorded history) there was not only light but television, satellites, electronic chips, high-speed and miniaturized computers, fiber optics networks, lasers, and the interlinks that comprise this Information Age: the potential for the greatest triumph of literacy, and the broadest exchange of ideas among peoples and nations.

But international affairs had not been nearly as revolutionized as international communications. In place of Nazi-Fascist utopianism there was Marxist-Leninist utopianism. Colonialism was too often replaced by neonationalist oppression in emerging countries with authoritarian regimes. The recuperating democracies, vying to secure markets abroad, dominated communications systems and conveyed mainly news that interested their primary audience, in the West. This economic competition was overshadowed, however, by the ideological/military challenges stemming from the Soviet Union. These challenges pitted collectivism (under centralist governmental control) against individualism (including competitive ownership of communications media) which was little regulated and weakly supported by democratic governance. Communications theory and systems matched the governance systems: communications were open and free-flowing when governments were free; under closed systems the media were government-controlled. When government oppression loomed, radio stations were the first targets for capture, and newspapers fell soon after.

In that postwar climate, national economic systems relied on ever speedier movement of economic data essential to banks, marketers and political leaders. In the eyes of the developing countries and the Soviet bloc, the major Western news services, particularly those four responsible for 90 percent of the global news traffic, reflected not only the record of the day's events, but also the interests of economic and political systems in which they were headquartered. By 1970, the communications media became increasingly the subject of attack by Marxist-Leninists and, for quite different reasons, by neonationalists. Every country, it was realized, needed communications for governmental intelligence and policymaking, as well as for communicating national news, culture and propaganda. Several Western countries were the headquarters for the dominant media systems.

By 1976 it would be assumed somewhat simplistically by journalists and their governments in Western Europe and

North America that the struggle was only between governmental censorship and press freedom--on a grand, universal scale. While Third World and Soviet critics did, indeed, chide the Western media for their links to the market systems, many developing countries had less controversial agendas. They sought better, more balanced coverage of their societies, the securing of their own communications facilities with the training to operate them as they pleased, and interlinks with major Western news services. In brief, these developing countries wanted to participate in the communications revolution.

Some Third World countries were, indeed, driven by restrictive notions. Censorship, or in today's cozier term, "news management," is endemic to government--all government. The important distinction is when maxi- or-mini-governmental control over information is justifiable, even in a democratic state, and when it is not.

That degree of difference is at the heart of the controversies, these past forty-five years, in international communications. Start with the easiest case: wartime press restrictions. (That debate between American journalists and the military was to flare up in 1983 when the U.S. intervened in Grenada, and left journalists behind.) American domestic and military censors proscribed much information during World War II. Paul Scott Mowrer, editor of the *Chicago Daily News* (and brother of Edgar Ansel Mowrer, the war correspondent who was one of Freedom House's founders), said: "In this nation of ours the final political decisions rest with the people. And the people, so that they may make up their minds, must be given the facts, even in time of war, or perhaps especially in time of war." This view was countered by a military censor at a meeting in Washington who stated, "I wouldn't tell the people anything until the war is over and then I'd tell them who won."

Press Responsibility

That inclination, in peace and war, afflicts all governments, even the most democratic. But there are dramatic distinctions. The U.S. government operated the Office of War Information as the civilian side of information control, and the Japanese government created the Patriotic Critics' Association and the Patriotic Commentators' Association to propagandize the Japanese people about war aims and achievements. But the Domei news agency and all Japanese newspapers and Radio Tokyo were converted into "public utilities" and given wartime missions. American media remained under private ownership, with the government providing broad guidance for military and security information.

The contrast between democratic and totalitarian journalism, even in a global war, was significant. Although no responsible American journalist would argue that reporters should reveal logistical and tactical information while life-threatening operations are in progress, censorship also can cost lives and lead to harmful policy and military mistakes. The censors in defense of U.S. policy for years forbade reporters to disclose the ineptness and defeats of the Chinese under Chiang Kai-shek. When that censorship broke down, it resulted in an all-too-favorable contrast from the Chinese Communist army under Mao Zedong, and the U.S. support for Chiang collapsed in 1944.

A clear statement of U.S. wartime censorship carries a moral today for that majority of the less-than-democratic countries that still controls news and information. Thirty years after war's end, in 1974, Charles Lynch, a Canadian correspondent with Reuters said it was "humiliating to look back at what we wrote during the war." He said, "We were a propaganda arm of our government. At the start the censors enforced that, but by the end we were our own censors. We were cheerleaders. I suppose there wasn't an alternative at the time. It was a total war. It wasn't good journalism. It wasn't journalism at all."

Such *mea culpa* notwithstanding, covering the battlefield, even with some censorship, can be journalism of the highest order. And there was much of that during World War II, as during other conflicts. The Vietnam war, two decades later, produced neither battlefield nor domestic censors. Correspondents were free to use military transportation to roam the countryside where combat was reported. The home front provided a field day for adversarial and investigative reporting. That was fed back to Vietnam where the domestic U.S. political threads were woven into the context of combat reporting; that fighting and how it was reported became a disruptive political and psychological factor in American society. The news media were frequently blamed for the social and political disruptions and the ultimate disintegration of U.S. policies in Vietnam. The media pushed press freedom to the limits, and beyond. Never before has a society so demonstrated its freeness in wartime. As a consequence, journalism seemed the white knight to those who opposed the war, and the irresponsible "estate," the loose cannon, to those who either supported war aims or felt the entire social fabric was being threatened by the mode of dissent that exploited dissent-reporting.

Not long after, during the Watergate affair, Americans were similarly divided over the role of the news media in bringing down a president. While they acknowledged that offenses had been committed in a high place, polls increasingly showed a loss of confidence in the news media. "Irresponsible" was used frequently to describe journalists who had "gone too far." Clearly, the newspapers in particular had broken new ground in extending the limits of investigative reporting.

Intelligence and military secrets never before revealed

Press Responsibility

were now on the front pages of newspapers. Early in 1986 the *Washington Post* learned the details of top secret U.S. intelligence gathering capabilities. This may have been the most vital information ever secured by a civilian journalist. Some of the information was revealed in the trial of a convicted spy, but the *Post* had more and indicated it would publish it. The paper voluntarily consulted defense and intelligence officials over several months. The director of Central Intelligence eventually threatened the *Post* with criminal prosecution if it published the story. President Reagan personally phoned Katherine Graham, chairman of the *Post,* with an appeal that the story not be published on national security grounds.

Said Benjamin Bradlee, executive editor of the *Post:* "We felt extremely uncomfortable with this information, but we had it, the Russians had it, and we asked why it should be kept from the American people." The *Post* said it was trying to frame a story that would "tell the American people what the Russians already knew, and only what they aleady knew."

The *Post* ran some of the story, withheld some. William Casey, CIA director, said "the media, as all other citizens, are responsible for knowing the law of the land." He added that "people ought to know their responsibilities. People ought to know when they're near the line." Who should be the judge? "It depends on the circumstance," said Casey. "If there is a law or a statute, as there is with respect to communications intelligence, the courts would be the ultimate determiners." The 1950 law, 18 United States Code 798, makes it a crime punishable by up to ten years in prison and a $10,000 fine to publish any classified information about devices used for communication intelligence. That is a rather specific legal restriction.

Should the mass media be excused on First Amendment grounds for breaching that law? Is there a public need to know the intimate details of intelligence matters, a purpose other than gaining titillation from a revealed secret? Is it a mark of press responsibility to see how close one can come to "the line"--the point of revealing truly vital information that can damage American security? Is not that a dangerous game and, even when cautiously played as in the *Post* case, one not worth the candle? It is likely, as the Hutchins Commission feared forty years ago, that intelligence leaking in the press will generate public support for greater governmental control of official information.

* * *

Though it is fashionable today for journalists to deny that intergovernmental organizations have the right to examine any issues of journalism, many basic concepts of press freedom may be traced to resolutions prepared and debated by Westerners at the League of Nations and in the United Nations system. The League considered international communications, including the news media, to be an acceptable subject for discussion within the framework of peacemaking and peacekeeping, the primary objective of the organization.

The full Assembly of the League on 25 September 1925 unanimously proposed convening journalists from "the different continents" to help organize peace by "ensuring the more rapid and less costly transmission of press news with a view to reducing risks of international misunderstanding" and "by discussing all technical problems, the settlement of which would be conducive to the tranquillization of public opinion." Such proposals at UNESCO in recent years were bitterly attacked by Western media and governments for mingling considerations of political objectives such as peace with (1) the content of journalism, (2) the need to improve communications technology particularly in developing countries, and (3) reducing the cost of news-media transmissions.

Similarly, in 1946 the charter of UNESCO included clear references to international communications as a channel for reaching a stipulated objective: peace, to be advanced through programs in education, science, culture and communications. The United States not only signed the UNESCO charter, but was one of its authors. Americans, notably Senator William Benton, a publisher, and Archibald MacLeish, Librarian of Congress, helped formulate UNESCO's principles and, particularly, the organization's commitment to raising the performance of news and other services in the interest of peace, "since wars begin in the minds of men." The UNESCO Charter would

> recommend such international agreements as may be necessary to promote the free flow of ideas by word and image...maintain, increase and diffuse knowledge...by initiating methods of international cooperation calculated to give the people of all countries access to the printed and published materials produced by any of them...[though UNESCO is] prohibited from intervening in matters which are essentially within...domestic jurisdiction.

The charter stated that a "peace based exclusively upon the political and economic arrangements of governments would not be a peace which could secure the . . .support of the peoples of the world." Therefore UNESCO's founders believed in "the unrestricted pursuit of objective truth, and in the free exchange of ideas and knowledge [and] are agreed and determined to develop and to increase the means of communication between their peoples and to employ these means for the purposes of mutual understanding and a true and more perfect knowledge of each other's lives."

That prophetic commitment (in the biblical sense) reflected the high idealism and appropriate rhetoric of the immediate postwar era. It is an idealism and rhetoric which should not be out of style today. Yet it may be, because the much enlarged constituency of UNESCO now places the Western inheritors of that idealism in the numerical minority; and the Soviet and neonationalist majority, in part, has used the UNESCO forum to discuss specific communications policies that sound idealistic but require governmental supervision and control of the *content* of messages. Western participants, consequently, seek to deny not only the valid complaints of Third World challengers of the dominant communications systems (including the news media), but reject even the restatement of the high prophesy of the Western founding fathers.

Western defenders, therefore, tend to turn instead to the brief, all-encompassing statement which appears as Article 19 of the Universal Declaration of Human Rights (1948). It speaks unequivocally about the desirable freeness of the flow of information:

> Everyone has the right to freedom of opinion and expression; this right includes freedom to hold opinions without interference and to seek, receive and impart information and ideas through any media and regardless of frontiers.

That unmodified support for uncensored domestic and international communications was softened in 1966 in the International Covenant on Civil and Political Rights signed by seventy states but not ratified by the United States. Its Article 19 repeats the declaration's commitment to freedom of expression, and even enlarges on the variety of media covered by the statement, but then goes on to say that this freedom "carries with it special duties and responsibilities." This has provided the opening for many subsequent efforts to specify the "duties" or, as a Soviet draft would have it, the "uses" of the mass media for particular objectives (advancing peace, opposing apartheid, etc.). This covenant also provides a further serious modification of the basic commitment. The rights granted may be "subject to certain restrictions, but these shall only be such as are provided by law and are necessary: (a) for respect of the rights and reputations of others [the democratic concept of libel law]; (b) for the protection of national security or of public order, or of public health or morals." These last modifiers, while reflecting the reality of ultimate state defense everywhere, are sufficiently broad to permit all manner of censorship by governments. Indeed, these limitations suggest the all-too-moral use of many forms of press controls. This is one of the reasons why even those Americans disposed to ratify the covenant would consider it only with strong formal reservations on this and similar articles.

In those formative years--the 20s and 30s at the League, and the 40s at the U.N. and UNESCO--votes were one-sidedly in favor of Rousseau, J.S. Mill, John Locke and Thomas Jefferson. After the arrival of scores of developing countries and the Soviet bloc had tilted the majority away from Western countries most of the time, consensual decision-making, granting every participant some veto-power, became popular. Consensual decisions inevitably produced a document that included concepts probably no signer would have written fully as accepted, but a statement nevertheless that all could live with.

Consensual documents created few if any problems for those governments with strong central control over their citizens, and particularly all domestic communications media. Such governments either withheld from their own people the passages deemed objectionable or they simply ignored or flouted such passages. The Soviet Union's signing the Final Act of the 1975 Conference on Security and Cooperation in Europe (the Helsinki Accords) is a glaring case in point. The third (human rights) basket of the accords specifies information exchanges, easing of journalistic travel, freedom to receive and exchange information--in addition to scores of human-contact provisions--that the Soviets have honored mainly in the breach. Worse still, they have meticulously harassed and imprisoned nearly all of the human rights activists inside the Soviet Union who tried to encourage their government to comply with the very accords the Soviets had signed in 1975. Such actions form the centerpiece of American and Western European criticism of the Soviet Union whenever the accords come under official review (as at Belgrade in 1977; Madrid in 1980-83; Ottawa, 1985; Budapest and Bern, 1986; and Vienna, starting in 1986). Retaining the Helsinki Process, then, is important in keeping the freedom (including the press-freedom) flame burning.

Yet some journalists, particularly editorial writers, believe that discussions of international communications, particularly press performance, have no place in the forums of intergovernmental organizations. They disregard the historic Western origin of the introduction of this issue into the League, the U.N. and UNESCO. In earlier times, it was thought that the role of journalists was enhanced by giving them a recognized function in the field of world affairs.

Truth is, mass communications--public and private data flows, news media, public diplomacy (broadcast and other public emissions)--have an essential impact on all governments and the citizens of all countries. Consequently, the fundamental role of journalism in society is now both recognized and challenged. Does the vital quality of journalism in society therefore require some new definition or even regulation in the public interest?

Press Responsibility

This is a question being asked not only in authoritarian or totalitarian countries. There, Marxist-Leninist dogma requires collectivist journalism exclusively in the interest of the state, in ways and under policies set by a small centralist elite. Neonationalist Third World doctrine, varying from country to country, often demands that domestic and foreign journalism be channeled through the governmental news agency. In both the Marxist and neonationalist systems the individual journalist is, in effect, a civil servant. Access to diverse news sources, and the expression of pluralist views are generally forbidden. The State has the news monopoly.

Countries with state monopolies often attack Western journalism as market or bourgeois "monopolies" and they add that Western journalism, though insisting that it is independent, is really linked intimately to the "ruling classes," and therefore the government itself. Soviet spokesmen, for example, could not believe that the newspapers that investigated the Watergate scandals, and that helped unseat a president, could have been other than a part of the ruling class carrying out orders to make an internal change predetermined by the same "class." Part of the French press, incidentally, had similar difficulty believing the U.S. press could help overthrow a president on what seemed to the French a relatively minor and not unusual sequence of political malfunctions.

Such observers apparently had improperly assessed one lesson developed during the Vietnam war: investigative reporting and the "new journalism" permitted the journalist far greater freedom to challenge authority, to set a public agenda for change and, by repeated reportorial coverage mingled with editorial-column support, to generate crucial changes in American policy. Pictorial and verbal reports inevitably changed the public attitudes--reduced the public support--for continuing American participation in the war.

In international forums in the 70s and 80s, critics of Western journalism proposed doing exactly what American reporters had often done during the Vietnam war: enlarge the right of individual journalists to investigate and write or speak as *they* decide, no matter what the view of the publisher or editor. This was called "democratic journalism." Such a process had, indeed, been apparent in the U.S. in the 60s and 70s, but *never* yet in the very countries demanding it in theory: the Marxist and neonationalist nations. There, only government monopolies prevail. And though they would insist that government journalists act always with a sense of "responsibility" for the interest of the State and, it would be added, the people, the fact is the people under authoritarian regimes have no control of the kind of information they want to receive through the mass media.

In the same international forums one hears demands for the "right to communicate" and the "right of access" to communicate. Both high-sounding terms appear to follow logically from the free-flow doctrine which the Americans and Western Europeans wrote into the earlier international charters. While the language is democratic-sounding the meaning is as aberrant as the reality of "democracy" in the several Peoples Democratic Republics of Europe, Africa and Asia.

Repeated misuse of an established term can soon give it new meaning. In the language of truly democratic journalism (i.e., independent of governments), "access" means the implied right of a reader or viewer to express views in the medium. There is, indeed, limited access now through letters columns of newspapers and magazines, and less regularly in radio and television. Those in the international arena who now demand "access" generally mean that the Western media should open their channels to replies by governments that feel they have been incorrectly or insufficiently reported by the mass media. That "right," in effect, would open the door for governmental regulation of the *content* of journalism in order to accept critical views from foreign citizens or governments. (It has been difficult for President Reagan to arrange even brief ceremonial exchanges over Soviet television, with no possibility of an American replying to previously aired Soviet views.) One thing is clear: Never again will the performance of the news media be free of critical analysis, and the politics of international communications.

The demand for access does, however, focus on a real problem in democratic states. There is little opportunity for the individual citizen to express views in the major print and broadcast channels. In that respect there is a monopoly of the journalistic profession. That is not to accept the Marxist or neonationalist charge that the private "monopoly" does not have the proclaimed commitment to "the people's" needs presumably found in governmental monopolies. The private marketplace of ideas still functions. Even the rapidly enlarging newspaper chains manage to retain some independence for the editorial writers and reporters subsumed in the buy-out of newspapers. There are, moreover, hundreds more suburban, regional, specialized and alternative papers today than forty-five years ago. And, of course, there are many magazines, paperback books, radio stations, and television systems that did not exist in 1941. While it is argued that the press and broadcasters generally set and follow the same agenda, this is the result not of conspiracy but rather the training of journalists to existing standards of style and newsworthiness. The competitiveness of private newsgathering also imposes time and space constraints which, in turn, homogenize reporting and coverage. The need to gain or hold an audience and/or *sell*--ads, time, or general acceptance--is bound to influence many news gatekeepers. Few will feature the longer-term, slower-"selling" story.

* * *

Yet most responsible journalists agree that the old search for the who? when? where? and what? of a story is no longer adequate. There is a professional commitment to seek balance within the story, and within the broader context in which the story takes place. That commitment also demands a certain inquisitiveness, or cynicism if you will, that leads to further questioning. But that same cynicism can also influence the writing or speaking of the reporter. It can also lead him to disbelieve all authority, especially corporations and the government, including a democratic government. It can lead to similar challenging of private citizens so that they lose their privacy, a right to be cherished. It can lead, then, to a public perception of the news media as seeking to be above the law, arrogant, the critics of all but subject to no criticism except their own limited editorial review.

Two public opinion polls in 1985 and 1986 attempted to quantify the degree to which the U.S. public had lost faith in the credibility of the American press. The 1985 study commissioned by the American Society of Newspaper Editors (ASNE) concluded that the U.S. press has a credibility problem. Many were said to feel that the press invades the privacy of ordinary people and shows disrespect for standard news sources. People generally identify with those being exploited by the press, the ASNE poll found, thus contributing to the distrust that diminishes press credibility. Credibility doubts were found among different kinds of people, including blacks, young people, and those at opposite ends of the socioeconomic spectrum. Inevitably,

Press Responsibility

ASNE feared, loss of credibility could lead to diminished press rights and privileges, as well as loss of readership.

A second poll in 1986, sponsored by the Times Mirror Company, declared that on the contrary "there is no credibility crisis for the nation's news media." It said that "if credibility is defined as believeability, then credibility is, in fact, one of the media's strongest suits."

The debate continues within the newspaper industry. Many findings were disturbing, no matter how favorably assessed. In the Times poll, 45 percent of respondents said news organizations were politically biased in reporting; 36 percent said this in the ASNE poll. In the Times study, 56 percent said news media are often influenced by powerful people and organizations; 36 percent said the same in the ASNE poll. Some 60 percent told Times interviewers that the media pay too much attention to bad news; a similar question asked for ASNE brought 65 percent agreement. Clearly, the long-term trend shows low public confidence in the U.S. press. A Harris survey in 1982 showed only 14 percent of Americans expressing confidence in the press, down from 28 percent in 1966. The confidence rating had risen to 19 percent in 1983, still far from reassuring.

The crediblity of the news media is a vital aspect of a free society. This was recognized in 1947 by Robert Hutchins and the high powered commission he headed to examine the performance of the U.S. press. The Hutchins Commission, in its own words, "set out to answer the question: Is the freedom of the press in danger? Its answer to that question is: Yes." The reasons given:

The importance of the press has greatly increased.

The few who have access to the machinery "have not provided a service adequate to the needs of the society."

"Those who direct the machinery of the press have engaged from time to time in practices which the society condemns, and which, if continued, it will inevitably undertake to regulate or control."

* * *

The commission used many terms and criticisms which have since surfaced in the international challenges to the Western news media. The commission called its report "A Free and Responsible Press." The term "responsible" is now regarded as a code word in international debates for agendas, some hidden, that would provide governmental determination of the end-product of communications: *content*. The commission presciently warned that government might intervene to "cure the ills of freedom of the press but only at the risk of killing the freedom in the process." Breaking up news conglomerates, however, said the commission, is not the same as breaking up an oil monopoly. Such action in the media field may destroy a needed public service. The commission recognized that news media have a basic right to independence. "The moral right of free expression achieves a legal status because the conscience of the citizen is the source of the continued vitality of the State." The commission acknowledged that "not every citizen has a moral or legal right to own a press or be an editor or have access [as] of right, to the audience of any given medium of communication." The commission immediately added this warning; "But it does belong to the intention of the freedom of the press that an idea shall have its chance even if it is not shared by those who own or manage the press." Plurality of views--if not plurality of ownership--is then the principal judge of whether a news medium is adequately informing the public of a democratic society. As if to underscore this, the commission added: "The press must be accountable to society for meeting the

Press Responsibility

public's need and for maintaining the rights of citizens and the almost forgotten rights of speakers who have no press." This warning becomes increasingly relevant as newspaper chains grow larger and the number of individually owned papers diminishes.

The commission expanded on the functions of mass media in a democratic state. The news media were said to be "an educational instrument, perhaps the most powerful there is; and they must assume a responsibility like that of educators in stating and clarifying the ideals toward which the community should strive." Shades of the later UNESCO debates on press responsibility! How this can be achieved was also discussed by the commission in 1947. The press was urged to "engage in vigorous mutual criticism" and, for example, establish "a new and independent agency to appraise and report annually upon the performance of the press." The commission warned that "the press must know that its faults and errors have ceased to be private vagaries and have become public dangers. Its inadequacies menace the balance of public opinions....The important thing is that the press accept the public standard and try for it. The legal right will stand if the moral right is realized or tolerably approximated. There is a point beyond which failure to realize the moral right will entail encroachment by the State upon the existing legal right."

The findings of the Hutchins Commission were quickly attacked and then buried by the American news media. The call for socially responsible journalism was particularly rejected by the professional journalists and their associations. Indeed, when the self-appraising National News Council was finally created in 1973 it was opposed by major newspapers and networks, and died in 1985. It had delivered a number of useful analyses of broad and narrow questions of journalistic practice and integrity. The major media, however, paid these findings little heed, and mainly reported only the council's demise.

Yet the theory of journalistic "responsibilty" remains a heated controversy in international forums. American journalists and government officials routinely reject the concept on the ground that only a journalist can determine what is responsible journalism, and a governmental discussion can only be for the purpose, expressed or not, of controlling the content of journalistic output. While granting that possibility, I would also hold that questioning the nature of journalistic responsibility, as well as press freedom, is a valid exercise. It depends entirely on *who* does the analysis, and for what purpose. For no societal institution, particularly in a free society, should be above public monitoring and analysis of its performance. Certainly there is no more vital institution of a free society than the news media. It is not sufficient to say that the marketplace weeds out the good from the bad. That may be true of egregious error, or small and aberrant publications. But the market process operates slowly and not with particularity. A single article may be blatantly biased, and the remaining pieces unobjectionable. How is a reader to respond? Letters may have some influence, but some publications do not carry readers' letters. Certainly television and radio carry little response from the audience. Letters directed to advertisers may have some effect, but not often. The pros can usually mount a letter campaign to counter the cons.

* * *

A definitive text addressing the changing need for higher journalistic responsibility was published in 1956 by Fred S. Siebert, Theodore Peterson and Wilbur Schramm. They set forth four models of the press: the authoritarian,

Press Responsibility

libertarian, Communist, and that reflecting social responsibility. The book quickly rejected the authoritarian and Communist modes. While the authors were favorably disposed to the libertarian model--let freedom of the press reign freely--they found it incomplete. They approved the absence of governmental controls but said there must be more to effective journalism in a complex democratic and industrial society. That "more" should be a pervasive sense of social responsibility demonstrated by the journalist as reporter, editor, broadcaster or publisher. Social responsibility implies concern for the consequences of journalistic activity. If a report would endanger the physical safety of individuals or the security of the nation, should it be made public without adequate safeguards to prevent dangerous consequences? Or, at another level, if media coverage undermines a private citizen's reputation, without some redeeming social value, should that be excused as the public's right to know? Perhaps still more important in the daily operation of the news media, should not long-range analysis of significant trends find a prominent place in daily reporting even if there are no immediate developments to record? That question is repeatedly asked by thoughtful citizens of developing countries who dislike Western coverage of coups and exotica at the expense of "process" stories based on deep-seated problems that will remain for a long time. Such "news" should be covered today, though it has not yet reached a crisis called newsworthy. Indeed, such coverage may help forestall a crisis, and be justification for exhibiting journalistic responsibility.

Stressing social responsibility, I believe, provides the necessary element that is missing in the traditional libertarian or press-freedom view. It is no longer sufficient, if it ever was, to expect journalists to ignore the great influence their work has on the lives of citizens, at home and abroad, and on the interaction of governments as a consequence of journalistic products. That's not to justify governmental control or even intergovernmental regulation in the setting of universal norms. In a world as divided as it is today, universal standards for journalists are not only impossible to achieve but would be as flawed as the dangerous assumption that the nonnegotiable--including freedoms of the journalist-- can somehow be negotiated: the not-free and the free compromising their differences.

The Prime Minister of Malaysia in 1985 tried to justify his country's less-than-free "guided journalism" as a fitting example of the exercise of "social responsibility" of journalists. He said that "an irresponsible press is a negation of the right of the people in a democratic society. If the press fails to understand this, then it should be made to do so by the people through their elected representatives." Dr. Mahathir Mohamad noted that "the concentration of media even in the United States, the haven of the libertarian model, have concentrated power in the hands of a select few." He asked: "How many truth-seeking newspapers and television stations will go into print or on the air with scattered bits of information in the knowledge that they are not in possession of the facts, still less all the facts, simply to beat their competitors? And for what? For the good of the individual, man and society?" He added that "the ability of the journalist to influence the course of events is out of all proportion to his individual right as a citizen of a democratic society. He is neither especially chosen for his moral superiority nor elected to his post." A free press, said the Prime Minister, "is as prone to corruption as are the other institutions of democracy." He asked: "Is this, then, to be the only institution of democracy to be completely unfettered?"

His conclusion is clear: "The media must be given freedom. But this freedom must be exercised with respon-

Press Responsibility

sibility. It must be given the freedom to express opinion freely, even the right to be wrong; but must do so without prejudice and without malice. Just as in a democratic society no person or institution has a right to destroy society or to destroy democracy, the media [have] no such right." Thus, "when the press obviously abuses its rights, then democratic governments have a duty to put it to right."

Putting the press "to right," however, may well obliterate the watchdog of government, and then democracy itself. The Prime Minister's government in 1986 has repeatedly acted to threaten restriction of the press, including severe strengthening of penalties under the Official Secrets Act. Yet the Prime Minister raises the ultimate dilemma for both the news media and democratic societies.

Information is power and, as with all power, news media can distort and destroy as well as inform and enlighten. Journalists reflect human limitations and frailties, as well as high skill, and personal and professional integrity. The business of journalism has marketability as a competitive goad; the profession of journalists invokes high personal and social standards of ethics and performance. The mundane tussles daily with the sacred.

It should not be surprising, then, that critics at home and abroad exhibit unease over the performance of the news media. The critics assess journalistic shortcomings against a prophetic, idealistic standard which can be realized only in some messianic age. Until that far-off day readers and viewers should press for ever-improving journalistic standards that are rigorously self-policing--and perceptively so to the public. Journalism schools and on-job training should instill in each practitioner a sense of social conscience, as well as professional and operational integrity. There should be a Pulitzer Prize for the journalist who best handled a sensitive situation, properly skirting the dangers yet telling the crux of a story. The government and the press are inevitably in a state of tension. The watchdog journalist will never be loved, but he can be respected for embodying the conscience of a good citizen, as well as the drive of a headline-maker. Criticism and correctives within and between the media should be conducted with the same diligence and probing investigation as journalists now critique every other human institution.

That suggests a higher and even freer form of journalism: the expectation that each practitioner, whether reporter, editor or manager, answer each day to a standard of performance which weighs the ultimate effect of the journalistic product, as well as the present factors of objectivity, balance, completeness and contextuality.

Perhaps that is what a majority of Americans has been seeking while rating the news media low in confidence and credibility, an expression of rising expectations of the citizen's "need to know."

"In the final analysis," said Michael J. O'Neill, former editor of the *New York Daily News*, "what we need most of all in our profession is a generous spirit, infused with human warmth, as ready to see good as to suspect wrong, to find hope as well as cynicism, to have a clear but uncrabbed view of the world. We need to seek conciliation, not just conflict--consensus, not just disagreement--so that society has a chance to solve its problems. So that we as a nation can find again the common trust and unity--so that we can rekindle the faith in ourselves and in our democracy--that we so urgently need to overcome the great challenges we face in the 1980s."

Computerization & Modern Society

John Diebold

Computers are no longer the strange, isolated and distant realm of glass-enclosed laboratories and basement data-processing shops. The technology that lets us store, process and disseminate information with astonishing ease has become ubiquitous, a fact of modern life. Computer-generated images and digitized voices have altered our perceptions of the world. Meanwhile, the speed, accuracy and efficiency of computerization have changed our expectations not only of machines but of people: we demand with ever greater impatience that services be quick and competent, that information be error-free.

The computer's presence is such a commonplace in our lives as to go almost unnoticed. Automated bank tellers cheerfully dispense our cash at all hours of the night, while grocery store cashiers scan our purchases with electronic "eyes." There remain few, if any, aspects of our lives that have not been in some way touched by the computer.

Computerization

The miniaturization of the computer's power onto tiny slabs of silicon was the crucial breakthrough that brought the technology into our homes, our automobiles, our offices. The same power that formerly required tons of computer hardware and thousands of vacuum tubes can fit handily onto one of these quarter-inch-square chips, driving all manner of consumer goods from dishwashers to sewing machines to wristwatches. It is a technology as near as the telephone, as pervasive as the satellites that beam down television signals from space. And for those who carry computerized pacemakers implanted in their chests, the computer is as fundamental as human life.

The visible artifacts of this new age--the personal computers and computer-driven appliances--are only the smallest of the many ways in which our society has been, and continues to be, transformed. For one who has spent an entire career advising businesses and governments on the implications of information technology, I have witnessed over a span of four decades the evolution of our society into what may truly be called the Information Age. The early irrational fears that computers and robots would somehow take over the world have largely disappeared, and the technology is overwhelmingly accepted as a force for good in today's world.

And yet, computers continue to raise the most basic ethical and moral questions: issues of privacy, liberty and human dignity. Although filled with optimism over the computer's promise, I am not one to dismiss the many legitimate concerns that have been raised over the computer's power. Like information itself, information technology is intrinsically neutral. Yet it can be used either for ill or for good; to liberate or to control.

While information has always been collected and manipulated for unethical and even malevolent purposes,

Diebold

there are two particular aspects of the computer that amplify the capacity for human harm. One is the great ease with which large volumes of information may be accessed and controlled. In the days when government information was collected in dusty filing cabinets, most of us were quite safe from encroachments on our personal privacy and liberty. It was neither possible nor practical for governments or any other organization to keep tabs on hundreds of millions of citizens. The computer has changed that: because of its ability to store mountains of data on small, compact records and to access any one of them with breathtaking speed, it is possible to learn effortlessly the minutest details of a citizen's life, from his spending habits to his psychiatric record to his employment performance.

This same ease of access makes possible a technique known as computer matching. Two cases in recent years caused particular concern to civil libertarians. In one it was revealed that the Selective Service System had cross-checked lists of draft registrants with records from the Social Security System and state motor vehicle registrations to identify young men who had failed to register for the draft. In another case, Internal Revenue Service files were matched against Welfare Department roles to pinpoint cases of welfare fraud: individuals whose high incomes should have disqualified them from welfare benefits.

Proponents of these computer matching techniques argue that their sources of information are all openly available. And yet, before the days of computers, it would have required an army of workers to have manually cross-checked Selective Service lists against all state motor vehicle registrations. Computers make it possible to do what was once inconceivable.

Beyond the ease of access affforded by this powerful machine, a second and more insidious aspect of the computer has perhaps even greater capacity for harm. I refer to the perceived infallibility of computers. Consider the case of Michael Ducross who, in 1980, was stopped by police in Huntington Beach, California, for making an illegal turn. Within seconds, the police had checked the FBI's computer records in Washington and found that Ducross was wanted for having gone AWOL from the Marine Corps eleven years before. He was held in prison for five months before it was realized that the computerized records were in error. Certainly if a single human being had levied the AWOL charge against Mr. Ducross, no one would have believed it before making cross-inquiries. And yet the information dispensed by computers was trusted almost blindly. Although it is rarely acknowledged, human errors--and occasionally machine errors--can occur in data processing. And those inadvertent errors may cause more havoc than the intentional misuse of computers.

Record-keeping blunders and the misuse of public information are certainly not new. But these problems have become matters of some immediacy as a result of advances in information technology which accelerate and broaden the potential for large-scale abuse.

What protection do citizens need from wrongful use of personal data? What should be the limits of government surveillance? What regulations should govern the use of information gathered by public agencies? Should information gathered for one purpose be allowed to be used for other purposes?

* * *

And what are the potential abuses associated with private data networks? Banks, credit companies, insurers, hospitals, professional groups and retail stores, to name a few, all carry detailed profiles on millions of citizens. One would have to be a kind of hermit--self-employed and self-sufficient, owning little in the way of personal property, paying for everything by cash or by barter--to escape from inclusion in the massive computer data banks.

Personal privacy can be compromised quite unintentionally through the offshoots of information technology. A report distributed by Knight News Service in 1979 told of a bank that had installed a network of automated teller machines. The bank discovered, on reviewing its computerized records, that an unusual number of withdrawals were made every night between midnight and 2:00 a.m. Suspecting foul play, the bank hired detectives to look into the matter. It turned out that the late-night customers were withdrawing cash on their way to a local red light district! The article observes that "there's a bank someplace in America that knows which of its customers paid a hooker last night." What uses might an unscrupulous bank employee have made of such information?

Must we sacrifice privacy for the conveniences of modern life? How can personal data be protected and controlled? And how can such control be restored to the individual citizen? We created the technology behind massive information systems. Can we not also create the technology--and the public policy--that will effectively restrict the dissemination of their contents?

On the flip side of the coin, we must remember when data collection is for the public good. The Reagan Administration had proposed in 1983 that the Census Bureau be allowed to share with other statistical agencies the demographic data that it collects. It was not a matter of whether those other agencies were entitled to the information; they were already gathering identical information on their own. It was simply a matter of elimi-

Computerization

nating redundant effort and making government more efficient. Later in 1983 the plan was killed in Congress, basically for fear of privacy intrusions. What savings might have accrued to the taxpayer if these overlapping data collection efforts were consolidated?

* * *

I first ran into this problem in 1951 when, as a student intern in what was then the Economic Cooperation Administration, I had spent a summer compiling trade statistics. By the end of the summer, I had a good first-hand feeling for the wasteful and duplicative process of gathering statistics from many government agencies and processing them. A dozen years later, in 1963, I paid a visit to President Kennedy's budget director, Kermit Gordon, who happened to have been my outside Honors Examiner in Economics at Swarthmore. I told him a little about computers--it is difficult today to comprehend just how strange and new computers were at that time--and I proposed to him that there be a central statistical bureau in government with a large computer data base, from which each agency could draw upon data as needed.

Gordon thought this a fine idea and he suggested I visit Ewan Clague, then commissioner of the Bureau of Labor Statistics. It was with great anticipation that I went to have lunch with Clague, a man I had regarded in school as something of a legendary figure. To my surprise, he reacted very emotionally to my idea. The reasons soon became obvious. Robert Kennedy had been pressing the Justice Department to use some of the data BLS had been gathering for compilation of their indices. Clague was adamant that any violation of his agreements with data suppliers as to the secrecy of their source would destroy the data's validity, and he told me he would resign his post if the attorney general prevailed. I am sure he was right, and I only then began to understand at least one aspect of the problem!

* * *

At what point do the costs of privacy protection outweigh the benefits? Without question, personal privacy is the essence of the human liberty on which our country is based. Privacy protection is a most worthy object of public policy. Although we can generally come to some consensus on the ends, there are no simple answers when it comes to articulating the means.

Can we find ways to streamline our government's data collection efforts, while still maintaining strict guidelines on the use of that data? My feeling is that we can. I believe human freedom has never been more assured than it is today, in the Computer Age. The source of my optimism is our society's growing sophistication and awareness of the computer's potential. Armed with that knowledge, citizens are best equipped to demand the highest standards of data collectors, whether they be credit agencies or elected officials. We must continue to encourage public debate on the issues posed by an information society.

We can never go back to the Luddite phobias that characterized the early days of computers. We have come a long way since Charlie Chaplin first documented our fears of a regimented, mechanized society in his film *Modern Times*. Today, the same Charlie Chaplin has become the hallmark of a new and "friendly" computer age: as the affable character in IBM personal computer advertisements.

Our future relationship with this awesome new technology is decidedly within our control. Much will depend upon an informed citizenry. It is only by under-

Computerization

standing the great positive potential that information technology represents--and by harboring no illusions of the dangers--that we can achieve the promise of an information democracy. And the computer itself is a powerful instrument in the building of an open and informed society. For example, interactive videotex technology will open live, two-way information channels between citizens and government bodies. It will thus be possible for citizens to participate more directly in government, to make their voices heard.

It is no wonder that totalitarian nations have worked so diligently to control the use of personal computers. Wherever individuals can touch the keyboards that link them with communication networks, people will have access to information. And those people will be free.

U.S. Intelligence: Yesterday, Today-- and Tomorrow

Leo Cherne

The functioning of United States foreign intelligence will remain seriously hampered until the American people better understand the nature of the role of foreign intelligence, the importance of its functioning, and its indispensability if peace is to be preserved. We must first halt and reverse the increasing cynical perception of intelligence activities as shameful, degrading. We must then build on more balanced judgements.

Today's and tomorrow's society differ in critical respects from the international military environment which essentially ended with World War II, soon after Freedom House was founded.

Among the forty-two current conflicts involving four million people engaged in wars, rebellions or civil uprisings, few nations have declared war upon another. This ambiguity about hostility today places a particular premium upon effective intelligence. One of the requirements for the late

U.S. Intelligence

80s is to confront the fact that among intellectuals there are those who are blind to an adversary that prohibits ideas. Peacemakers exist who are uncritically ready to serve a perpetual war-making machine. Journalists develop myopia when confronted with a system that prohibits the freedom of the press. Writers fail to be outraged by a mechanism which corsets and commands the writer. Civil libertarians are slow to criticize a system that most completely obliterates civil freedoms. Celebrated artists remain blind to a system from which artists flee.

It is said that Marxist-Leninism as an ideology no longer exerts the appeal it once did. In a sense that's true. Nevertheless, each of the previous paradoxes remains. They are no longer expressed by yesterday's adulation of the USSR. Today they are found in a constant and undiminished opposition to those who would keep the Kremlin's dangerous propensities in check. For many people, in short, *we*, not *they*, are the enemy.

We have recently been exposed to the shame of a number of Americans who sold some of our most sensitive intelligence information to the Soviet Union and other foreign governments. It appears that they betrayed their country not out of Marxist-Leninist convictions but for substantial monetary rewards. What is not publicly acknowledged today is that such betrayals are one consequence of neutralizing public support of intelligence, if not in fact portraying it as a shameful activity. Such a portrayal removes the element of shame and betrayal which should to some extent inhibit those who seek easy cash or who act out neurotic impulses that are not ideological but deeply personal. One of the intelligence tasks that confront us requires that public indignation against the traitor accompany his dishonor. Legal punishment may prove far weaker than social indignation and contempt.

I regard this aspect of our intelligence requirements for the remaining years of this decade as so important that I will elaborate at the sacrifice of detailing some of the specific tasks which must be performed by the intelligence community. It is essential to that enlarged role of intelligence that it be understood by the media and the public, and that its essential role be accepted. Let me restate that role:

The primary purpose of intelligence is to avert war by alerting us to any dangers to our national security. The second role of intelligence is to help us to make the wise judgments needed to retain our strength--military, political and economic--against the many threats to each of these. (We must be clear that some of these dangers will grow in the years ahead.)

We are living in a world in which our interdependence increases more quickly than our ability to assimilate its significance. That interdependence involves manufacture and trade, commodities and credit communications, vital resources and ideas. It also stimulates tensions between nations and instability within them. The technological developments that have revolutionized world banking and the transfer of credit are fraught with consequences which cry for prompt and accurate assessments. We are dependent increasingly, even for our vital sources of military strength, on capabilities and resources which are diminishing here and increasing elsewhere.

Intelligence is an indispensable tool that enables us to understand the consequences of this rapid movement to a profoundly changed and interdependent world, that enables us to devise policies that enhance our ability to shape our destiny.

The essence of the difference of intelligence in the democracies and in the Marxist-Leninist states is that the normal purpose of our foreign intelligence is to buttress

U.S. Intelligence

stability, to make change as unturbulent as possible. It essentially seeks to protect the democratic order. And its errors and biases tend toward the maintenance of the status quo--on occasion a flawed status quo.

The KGB's role is almost the precise opposite, except within its political domain. Its function is to generate and exploit turbulence. "The worse, the better" is an old Russian nihilist maxim which aptly describes the nihilist thrust of Leninist intelligence activities wherever stability exists. The Soviet intelligence apparatus is inherently the provocateur, the merchant of disorder, the magnifier of social, economic or political weakness or distress. It is the ultimate force which enhances the possibility of conflict, careful only that the flames ignited not singe the flame thrower.

One of the requirements for the late 80s is to confront the fact that there are among intellectuals those who are blind to an adversary that prohibits ideas. Peacemakers exist who are uncritically ready to serve a perpetual war-making machine. Journalists develop myopia when confronted with a system that prohibits the freedom of the press. Writers fail to be outraged by a mechanism which corsets and commands the writer. Civil libertarians are slow to criticize a system that most completely obliterates civil freedoms. Celebrated artists remain blind to a system from which artists flee.

The massive lethal power possessed by the great nations--and most particularly the United States and the USSR--has had a still inadequately understood effect upon warfare. Smaller nations are infinitely more free to take belligerent action than are the two muscle-bound giants. This does not mean that we are equally paralyzed or that the United States and the USSR adapt to this reality similarly. The belligerent propensities of smaller nations all too often involve the interests of the superpowers and, somewhat less often, the participation by a superpower by means short of war. How, where and why such indirect intervention occurs is a crucial difference between us. So, too, is the freedom or eagerness with which the superpowers engage in such indirect action.

* * *

The Soviet Union has pressed to the hilt the use of proxy nations to perform its purposes--content to rely on our fear of wider war to keep us largely paralyzed. Within this rubric we have seen the growth of a new form of war--terrorism--supported, if not spawned, by nations virtually secure in the absence of risk to themselves. Such involement is almost invariably supported by the Soviet Union and its client states. Joint action to punish those who unleash terror is not as invariably supported by our allies. In fact, it is frequently shunned.

There will be no more difficult task for intelligence in the years ahead than to penetrate the small fanatic groups which perform the terrorist acts, groups that are utterly without moral restraint and that hold the innocent in complete contempt. But that intelligence task will become nearly impossible if we do not understand that terrorism is itself simply another form of warfare.

One of the most penetrating and accurate descriptions of the true nature of terrorism was contained in a statement that emerged from a conference on "State Terrorism and the International System," held under the auspices of the International Security Council in Tel Aviv not long ago. Sixty prominent senior statesmen, active and retired military officers and national security specialists from twelve countries convened to consider the character and extent of state-sponsored terrorism. Among their conclusions, the following are particularly penetrating.

U.S. Intelligence

The problem indeed is not just loose, gang-like incursions. It is terrorism--state-sponsored, state-supported, state-condoned, and even state-directed. Tyrannical and totalitarian ideologies have now subscribed to a new gospel of violence as an instrument of political change. A "Radical Entente" presently spearheaded by five militant states (Syria, Libya, Iran, North Korea and Cuba) is making coordinated efforts--by themselves and with others--to undermine the power and influence of the United States and its allies. Here the well-documented role of the Soviet Union is to provide the professional infrastructure of terrorism, including money, arms, expolsives, recruitment and training, passports, infiltration and escape routes, transport, communications, safe havens, control officers, and more. Taken together, these constitute an elaborate international network of support systems for terrorists.

This is not to suggest that the Soviets push the buttons and that their hand is always, directly or indirectly, in play. None of us subscribe to that kind of over-simplification. But they do not initiate it, they encourage it. The destabilization and subversion have a pattern which serves Soviet interests, and this must be faced by leaders of the Free World even if, for the moment, it is not high on the official diplomatic agenda. Both lives and liberties are at stake. We must learn more about what we are dealing with--and do more about it.

Meanwhile the Soviet Union has pursued twin objectives during all the years since World War II's end: to separate the United States and Western Europe while mounting a relentless, sophisticated and surprisingly effective propaganda campaign to persuade the world that peace is the USSR's true purpose and that the risk to that peace resides in Washington, not Moscow. And the Soviet Union has perfected the manipulation of proxy bodies essential to the propagation of that all too widely accepted fantasy.

A great danger to stability is surprise. It is the vital attribute of terrorism and aggression. Intelligence is our only available instrument to keep these disasters in check.

Terrorism provides the clearest spotlight with which to illuminate the true purpose of intelligence. There are many vocal critics of our intelligence efforts. Almost none, however, includes in his distaste intelligence efforts designed to alert us to impending terror or to identify the terrorist perpetrators once they have struck. Yet in no respect is the function of intelligence, whether analytic or clandestine, different when applied to the frightful consequences of terrorism than when applied to other international hazards, some of which involve the threat to life and human safety which are infinitely greater.

I earlier referred to a contribution of intelligence that will be of increasing importance with each passing month of the years ahead: to protect not only our nation's freedom, security and stability, but to enhance the safety and stability of all the nations that seek to avert war and cultivate their own growth with minimal risks to their own tranquility. It is here that the rapid growth of interdependence is especially relevant. Let me list a few of the major dangers in which intelligence is an indispensable tool.

A decision was made by a handful of men which led to a reduction in the price of oil--price reduction by more than a third in less than a month. The life and death of nations and their economies will rest on how low that price falls. Some nations will benefit. Others face almost unmanageable social and economic turbulence. The consequences to us in the U.S. are many. Some of the possibilities: jeopardy for a number of U.S. banks; serious hardship for some industries and many localities; an economic fire storm that could overtake all of us. Only wise and sometimes swift government policy provides the possibility of moderating such consequences--and policy formation will be at least partially blinded in the absence of effective intelligence.

A number of less-developed nations are now indebted to banks, government and international institutions by an amount in excess of 900 billion dollars. It is less the debts than the consequences that flow from their payment or nonpayment of the interest on those debts that hold a world in thrall.

It is unfortunate that many of those now in debt are countries that only recently adopted democratic governmental forms. Political and social instability in those countries can swiftly snuff out that recent progress and the danger may be as close as our own southern border. The meeting of the five leading finance ministers of the industrial nations illustrates the urgency of cooperative international policy, and intelligence is an indispensable mapmaker of the charts needed to navigate these shoals.

* * *

We have entered the age of high-technology married to the information age of the microchip, super-computer, and the new sophisticated robots known undramatically as "flexible means of production." Labor-intensive industries will continue to die or adjust, move their operations to countries which suddenly enjoy comparative advantage, or merge with successful foreign competitors.

There are virtually no American automobiles made entirely of American-made parts. The five leading Japanese car makers are all now operating on our soil. Television brings to every American home the news of cheap cars from East Europe and the Far East.

There are all the makings of international tension in

these facts--of disappearing American manufacture, of growing U.S. manufacturing unemployment. And the mix is one which threatens the growth of protectionism. And all this is grist for governmental policies that will be increasingly dependent on accurate and early intelligence.

Some of the best work on this process of structural change is being done by analysts in the CIA augmented by expertise derived from conferences, many of them unclassified, with business, universities, think-tanks and other groups.

Of what importance is this? Most observers who have studied the structural change I have referred to think that we are entering the greatest threshold of destabilizing change in the history of man--greater than the change set into motion with the birth of cultivated agriculture, greater than the industrial age which followed, greater than mass manufacture, greater than the birth of the service economy which now provides more than 70 percent of our jobs. We have entered the age of information and we will wander through it blindly unless effective intelligence helps shape prompt, effective and peaceful policy. Without it there is the greater certainty of turbulent and divisive economic conflicts.

The fact that I have concentrated on intelligence requirements for the balance of this decade may leave the misleading impression, especially in areas involving the dramatic economic difficulties we are likely to face, that the intelligence community is or should be the sole source of the information and judgment required for wise and timely government policy. It is clear that in specific fields and on a number of the potential difficulties that lie ahead, the Department of the Treasury, the Department of State, the Federal Reserve Bank, and the Department of Commerce, each have specific responsibilities which are assisted by sophisticated sources of information available to them.

U.S. Intelligence

Contributions made by the intelligence community to those key government agencies are on the one hand supplementary and on the other indispensable. Not only must each of these instruments of the federal government seek to improve its own sources of advanced knowledge and judgment, not only must the intelligence community make a unique contribution to that knowledge, but it may well be that the greatest contribution which may be required in the interval ahead is one which addresses itself to more effective coordination of sources of intelligence without which the policy responses may prove inadequate or late.

There are other very specific intelligence tasks which will be of increasing importance for the balance of this decade. Some of them are altogether new. Regrettably, almost none of them is easy. Yet they are indispensable. I'll refer to them briefly.

Among the urgent tasks for intelligence will be to fathom the means by which the Soviet Union intends to derive the benefits of the information age while withholding from its managers the technology and the freedom to use it, both of which are essential to eminence in the revolutionary structural change taking place.

Linked to the challenges of the information age, a host of intelligence questions emerge from the convulsive demographic changes taking place in the Soviet Union. These changes are shifting the balance of population to Moslem Russia and away from the shrinking population of Mother Russia where its government, industry and education are concentrated. By what means will the USSR attempt to cope with these ethnic tensions in European and Asian Russia?

Is it possible that the Soviet Union chose to buy and steal the high technology it requires because it is easier and cheaper to do that than to invent and produce their own high-tech breakthroughs? Their technical ability is surely not the total impediment. The spread of high technology capability in the Third World increases the difficulty of averting a transfer of sensitive technology to the Soviet Union. And this too will complicate the task for intelligence.

This new environment suggests still another need which partially involves intelligence and partially the continuous planning for industrial mobilization which is the Defense Department's responsibility. That question is: How do we manage our economy in an emergency when we are increasingly dependent on strategic materials, facilities and processes in other nations that may or may not be amenable or reliable when needed?

There is still another intelligence question which addresses itself to the periodic difficulties we have in securing participation by our allies in some of the international problems we confront. Perhaps the most striking illustration of this question is that nations that have suffered much more destruction of life and property at the hands of terrorists than has the U.S. appear quite unwilling to associate themselves with us in any action to redress state-sponsored terrorism.

Do we really understand why this is so? Are we altogether clear why neutralism and unilateralism play as large a role as they do in Europe? May not the distaste that many Europeans have for us exist because they correctly perceive the Soviet danger and correctly judge that they cannot moderate that danger, while we, by opposing the Soviet Union, might involve them in a risky and costly hazard they are not prepared to assume?

Can we win the war of systems if we cannot win the war of ideas or are unwilling to pay for what it takes to do so? The Soviet Union spends far more to jam VOA, BBC, *Deutsche Welle* and *Radio Francais* than the United States

U.S. Intelligence

and its allies together spend in efforts to reach the Soviet Union.

* * *

Among the tasks facing intelligence for the balance of this decade, pressing even at this moment, is the redefinition and legitimization of covert action. The alternative is to accept the notion that covert action is legitimate if used by the USSR, its client states, as well as the states which sponsor terrorism, but unacceptable as a counterforce to be used by the United States. We are no longer in Henry Stimson's world, in which, as he said, "gentlemen do not read each others' mail," or George Kennan's world in which, he said, "if covert action cannot be kept secret, it must not exist."

Closely linked to this, a fresh assessment must be made of the consequences of sharply limiting--or not limiting--the presence of the KGB on our soil. The Soviet Union's pervasive capabilities for telephonic eavesdropping enjoy immunity among us, and they operate from key urban locations. How can genuine symmetry be achieved in the privileges the Soviet Union enjoys among us and those they accord us in their midst? This is a major challenge which will continue to bedevil U.S. intelligence.

If the USSR has long been permitted to enjoy a field day in the U.S. it should be noted that they have not had uninterrupted success in many areas under their influence.

We must better understand what is producing Soviet distress among its clients elsewhere in the world and particularly in Africa. That distress varies, but it has infected Egypt, Somalia, Mozambique, South Yemen and Tanzania. There are now several on-going insurgencies fighting against Soviet-backed Marxist regimes; the wave of the future is not assuredly theirs.

Do we periodically subject our most certain conclusions and cherished conceptions about our adversary to remorseless re-examination? For example, are we too ready to assume that the Soviet Union's economic problems significantly diminish the continuing danger that Soviet power and will pose to our security?

It is clear that the tasks which lie ahead for intelligence are both different and greater than any which the intelligence community has previously confronted. There will be many problems in dealing with this painful reality. Almost all of them are affected significantly by the public's misconceptions, let alone repeated evidence of media hostility. There are problems which are bureaucratic; others which are budgetary. There are problems which flow from the very nature of a democratic state and some which flow from the peculiarly American culture. We have a remarkable tendency to look at the mirror when we consider our adversaries, and mirror-imaging is the curse of accurate intelligence.

We must also ask: can our intelligence be as good as it must be as long as our knowledge of foreign languages and cultures remains as poor as it is, especially when that handicap is further compounded by the disinvolvement of our centers of learning, research, science and technology, some of whom shun "contaminating" contact with the world of intelligence?

* * *

I conclude with a prophecy and a challenge. One is unavoidable and the other as yet unmet.

The prophecy: Less than fifty years ago, this nation, unlike England, had no need for economic intelligence. Whatever intelligence we had was focused on the capabilities and intentions rooted in dangers we perceived to be military.

U.S. Intelligence

During the remainder of the decade, I submit that the greater threats to stability will flow from hazards which are economic, social, cultural and political. I am not suggesting that the military dangers have receded. They have changed their character, but they are painfully still with us. However, a new panoply of dangerous troubles creates urgent intelligence needs in the years immediately ahead.

Now the challenge! The actors in this new international drama are not only governments; they include industries, labor unions, universities, banks, stock and commodity exchanges. Intelligence has thus far been essentially limited to informing other government sectors. We impose understandable limits, and they are sharp, to keep the world of foreign intelligence and our domestic life apart. We also have our antitrust laws. We do not, as the Japanese do, have an instrument like MITI which performs some of the coordinating and judgmental functions for Japanese industry.

Yet, how are we to meet the manifold challenges of the Information Age? How are we to share essential intelligence with the private sectors of our society, the sectors upon which tomorrow's eminence depends? Even were that intelligence to be shared, there remains the central problem that exists even in the most urgent governmental use of intelligence--how to make effective use of the information? By informing a man about to be hanged of the exact size, location and strength of the rope, you do not remove either the hangman or the likelihood of his being hanged.

All that intelligence can do is seek to concentrate the mind sufficiently to reduce the chance of unanticipated crisis, or, more hopefully, and less likely, avert it altogether. But if we are to continue to secure those freedoms we now enjoy, we will need that intelligence.

Religion, Morality & Public Values

James Finn

One cannot fully understand America and its freedoms without understanding the shaping influence that religion had and continues to have in this country.

Novus ordo seclorum. A new order of the age. It was historically new, in this new order, to declare that freedom of conscience, of belief, is an inalienable right. It exists above and beyond the power of the state to grant or to retract it. This principle of religious freedom is enshrined in the First Amendment to our Constitution: "Congress shall make no law respecting an establishment of religion, or prohibiting the free exercise thereof." This principle has been the source of continually unfolding implications that have then informed our political and social processes. This is also true of the implications lodged in the other half of that clause, which prohibits an established or preferred church.

It is a peculiarity of our republican government that it

Religion

depends for its informing vitality on resources that it does not itself possess and that it cannnot command. Most of the founders of this country believed that the political system they devised was a good system, but they also thought that it could be corrrupted by bad men. To function as it could and should, it needed the infused values of flesh and blood people. These values, they asserted, would be largely derived from religion. Theirs has remained a strong though not uncontested belief through most of our history. What these values are today, however, what religious communities most legitimately communicate them, and whether our society wishes to abide by them have become issues for intense debate.

The combination of religion and politics is reputedly potent. So it has proved in this country. Simply to mention some of the notable issues on which religious forces have exerted a strong if not controlling pressure is to confirm this truth: the anti-slavery movement, the temperance movement leading to legal prohibition, the civil rights movement of the 1960s, the opposition to the war in Vietnam, and the many rough, informal debates that were, in fact, religious tests for political office, including the presidency. These events also confirm that the course religion has traced through our history has run as smooth as true love, i.e., not very. The debates on these issues also substantiate the continuing truth of de Tocqueville's observation that in America the preachers talk like politicians and the politicians talk like preachers.

Although religion has provided values, vision, ritual, vocabulary, purpose, energy and cohesion to our society, it has also, on occasion, been divisive and has exacted high social costs. Religious leaders and their communities have not only been at odds with societal forces that they regarded as antipathetic to moral values, they have frequently been at odds with each other. Given the strong positions that religious groups are now taking on debated domestic and international issues, there is no reason to think that this will soon change. We are, in fact, in the very center of a national debate over which principles should direct our social vision. We can, however, reduce some of the costs, dilute some of the most corrosive fears, and better realize some of the benefits of that debate if we better understand the quite distinctive and pervasive role that religion occupies in our society.

"America," observed G.K. Chesterton, "is a nation with the soul of a church." More recently, Justice William Douglas described us as "a religious people." Despite sporadic discoveries of the death of God--considered ontologically, sociologically or politically--these personal evaluations are supported by a host of indices. More than 90 percent of the American people associate themselves with some religious faith. More than 40 percent attend Sabbath and Sunday religious services. After declining for some time, the percent of young people who express serious interest in religion is increasing. To the surprise of those whose concern it is to anticipate deep societal trends, the advance of modernity and its attendant forces has not been followed by secularization and a consequent decline in religious observance. In this respect, as in a number of others, America continues to confound ready expectation. We are not an easy people to understand.

One of the reasons that many people underrate the importance of religion in our national life is that it is so frequently ignored or poorly interpreted in our major media. With some notable exceptions, the media elite bring to their commentary on religion an intellectual sophistication that falls far short of that which they bring to politics, the arts, economics or sports. That religion fails to get the attention and consideration commensurate with the importance it has

Religion

in the lives of the American people is not the result of conscious design; it is, rather, the natural consequence of the media elites' lack of interest in religion. For the religious profile of this elite is in marked contrast to that of the American people. In a survey that was both extensive and intensive, S. Robert Lichter and Stanley Rothman found that 50 percent of the media elite declare that they have no religious affiliation and 86 percent attend religious services seldom or never. The result is that, in regard to religion in American life, many in the media are perpetually virgin, temporarily losing their innocence when religion thrusts itself into their societal consciousness, but marvelously recovering their innocence after the event.

This lack of intellectual sophistication in matters religious is not only regrettable, it is deleterious to our national self-understanding. There have been, in the last several decades, profound religious changes in this country and these changes resonate within our entire political and social structures. The significance of these changes should not be the interest and possession of academics only. The meaning and implication of these changes affect all of us and should be available to all of us. We remain ignorant of them at our cost.

The profound religious changes can be summarized as a realignment of forces within the larger religious community itself. The major elements of that realignment are (1) the decline of the long-dominant Protestant establishment (2) the increased legitimacy of Catholicism in this country (3) the decision of evangelicals and fundamentalists to engage strenuously in the political arena (4) a strong revival within the branches of American Judaism, and a shifting set of Jewish-Christian alliances.

To deal with these briefly in turn. From its founding, this country had a strong Protestant cast. Relatively free of much of old world inheritance--of feudalism, of Reformation and counter-Reformation, of anticlericalism--America developed a political and social structure open to all religions, but one dominated by Protestants. That de facto establishment communicated an ethic, struck a tone, and provided the necessary legitimacy for the new society. Our culture became, in many ways, a Protestant culture informed by a Protestant ethic to which other, immigrant cultures were subordinated or alien. (The remarkable system of Catholic parochial schools developed precisely to escape that influence in the public schools.) It was assumed that the Protestant establishment would occupy the positions of leadership--cultural, educational, commercial, political--in our society. Although that establishment still exists, is still highly influential, and its icons are present on ceremonial occasions, it is a diminished presence; the former dominance is gone. The process of the decline has been long, but the present symptoms are unmistakably visible.

Our society has become increasingly pluralized and so have our elites. The easy hold that the Protestant elite had on cultural and social issues has been weakened, if not broken, by the rise of other elites. True broadly, this is also true in a narrower institutional sense. What are termed--now anachronistically--the mainline churches no longer reign as once they did within the religious communities, nor, in fact, do the leaders of these churches always lead their own constituencies.

A prime example of the disjunction between proclaimed leadership and actual influence is provided by the National Council of Churches (NCC), an umbrella organization formed in 1950 to coordinate the efforts of the mainline churches as they addressed social issues. Like many organizations, the NCC was invigorated by the social ferment of the 60s. Having adopted the slogan, "The world

Religion

should set the agenda for the church," the NCC, according to its critics, then looked at the world through the eyes of George McGovern. The result is that it has for years adopted positions well to the left of the political center. It has regularly denounced both domestic and foreign policies of the Reagan administration, charging that the administration denies that people are entitled to human services, that it props up assorted repressive regimes, that it is prepared to kill great numbers of people in order to impose its imperial will. The NCC dilligently spread this message even as members of the denominations represented in the NCC helped elect Ronald Reagan to the presidency. Dissatisfaction with the way the NCC translates its religious views into political positions is evident both in direct attacks on that organization and in its shrinking budget. A narrower example is provided by Riverside Church in New York, a church with a distinguished history and a record of extensive civic influence, whose present pastor played host, during the dog days of 1986, to Daniel Ortega, Nicaragua's president.

While such examples could be easily multiplied, one could readily give examples of ministers as well as laity in Protestant denominations who do not follow this path and who are seriously engaged in a re-examination and renewal of their religious mission and their social goals. But they are often doing so within a bureaucratic climate that makes their task a difficult one.

* * *

The question naturally arises. If the traditional Protestant establishment has lost its ascendency, what is poised to take its place? The answer is by no means clear. An obvious candidate is the Roman Catholic Church, the largest religious denomination in the United States. It is not

Finn

only the size of the church that suggests this possibility but the fact that the Catholic church in this country has attained a new assurance in recent decades and has developed a new, activist spirit.

An anecdote: In 1960, John Cogley, a former executive editor of *Commonweal*, a liberal Catholic weekly, and a former religion editor of the *New York Times*, is working at a center directed by Robert Hutchins, a member in good standing of the high Protestant establishment. Cogley had helped on the crucial speech that candidate John Kennedy had given to a group of skeptical Protestant ministers in Texas, a speech that marked a turning point in his presidential campaign. Knowing this, Hutchins says to Cogley after Kennedy's election: "Well, maybe now you'll be named Postmaster General." "No, " Cogley immediately replies, "we give that job to Presbyterians now." For once, the articulate Hutchins is at a loss for words.

A gloss on the anecdote: The Postmaster General was at that time a political appointee, and the position was traditionally awarded to Irish Catholics who had worked diligently to elect a Democratic president, (who was at least culturally Protestant). Hutchins had not recognized, as Cogley quickly did, that the election of a Catholic president confirmed, rather than initiated, a significant shift in the circulation of elites in this country. That shift marked a change in the cultural identity of who was appointed to high posts--and who did the appointing.

If the election of the first Catholic president confirmed the full cultural legitimacy of American *Catholics* in this country, the Second Vatican Council (1962-1965) confirmed the maturity of *American* Catholics in the universal church. That council adopted a decree that affirmed religious liberty, full freedom of conscience, as a basic human right. This document was largely the work of America's most distin-

Religion

guished Catholic theologian, John Courtney Murray, S.J. American Catholics learned that they could contribute more than loyalty and funds to the universal church, that their American experience allowed them to make a distinctive theological contribution.

The newly won assurance of American Catholics was coupled with the Vatican Council's directive, addressed both to clergy and laity, to promote actively the works of social justice. The result is a church that is prepared to engage even more energetically the great social issues of our country and our time. In the past, the Catholic church, while not passive or indifferent, was more circumspect than were activist Protestant denominations on the domestic issues it addressed, and it was content to leave foreign policy decisions to the secretariat in Rome. Now the Catholic church in this country speaks out forcefully on a host of issues, including foreign affairs. Catholic bishops and those who speak for them have addressed such issues as abortion, racism, poverty, unemployment and capital punishment; they have frequently criticized U.S. policies in Latin America, have questioned many of our defense policies, and have found the profit motive in multinational enterprises a vexing issue.

Some of the developed statements of the National Council of Catholic Bishops, (NCCB) have drawn both warm support and at least equally warm criticism. Their 1983 pastoral letter on war and peace is a case in point. That letter is the single best document on morality and modern war produced by any religious denomination in this country-- alas! For it is seriously flawed. Both supporters and critics agree that it highlights serious moral issues, but the former regard its guidelines for policy as sound while its sometime critics (among whom I am one) believe that if those guidelines were pressed into service they would seriously weaken the defense of the U.S. and its allies. One of the authoritative interpreters of this pastoral letter says that its moral acceptance of our deterrent system rests on a "centimeter of ambiguity," and a number of bishops would withdraw even that centimeter. But even its critics cannot--or should not--slight the impact the letter has had. (Effective within the Catholic community, it has also inspired analogous efforts within Protestant denominations. The bishops of the United Methodist Church, for example, have produced a document that declares our deterrent system to be "the unquestioned idol of national security.") The Catholic bishops' pastoral letter on the U.S. economy is destined to provoke similarly divided reactions. Both flow from a particular moral and political view of the world that is sympathetic to detente, some manifestations of liberation theology and the socialist aspirations of Third World countries. And on these matters there are large divisions in the church.

    The disagreements over such episcopal statements only suggest, however, the many differences that exist among Catholics on a wide range of issues, some trivial, but many profound. They range from matters of war and the economy to those of the liturgy, abortion, feminism, divorce, gay rights and the ordination of women. The casual observer of the Catholic church could be forgiven for thinking that a religious monolith (which it never was) has been trans-formed into a tower of Babel (which it is not yet). An incisive social critic, the Lutheran minister Richard John Neuhaus, has stated that, in American terms, this may be "the Catholic moment." Whether it is or not will depend on whether the church can gather its scattered forces behind a vision that evokes support from many Americans--including many who are not Catholic.

    A third remarkable event on the religious scene today

Religion

is the rise of fundamentalism as a political and social force to be reckoned with. Without nuance, fundamentalists can be described as the right wing of conservative Protestantism. Traditionally directing their attention to issues of personal morality such as drinking, smoking, gambling and fornication, they shied away from "worldly" issues. Now they are in the thick of such issues, even producing potential candidates for high political office. They have entered the political arena, however, not because they have deserted issues of personal morality but because they now see such issues as the substance of our current culture and the object of recent legal rulings that they do not like. In their expressed view, the mass media have almost casually accepted and transmitted permissive attitudes toward drug use, premarital sex, deviant sex, pornography and non-traditional attitudes toward family roles and responsibilities. They see the Supreme Court in *Roe v. Wade* as setting aside abortion laws of fifty states and interrupting--without actually settling--an ongoing national debate on an issue that arouses their deep beliefs and passions. It is the same Court, they feel, that also ruled against all prayers in schools. The fundamentalists say that their values, many of which had recently been the general values of our society, are not only being rejected but scorned. They understand "secular humanism"--a term used to encompass a large set of current values and practices--to be the chief cultural danger and therefore their chief antagonist.

Provoked into going public, fundamentalists have resorted to techniques that were long familiar to other organized groups, secular and religious: to lobbying, polling, exhorting, marching, fund-raising, and employing the mass media, including radio and television, as best they can. This essentially defensive, or reactionary, campaign drew often horrified responses from those who perceived--quite accurately--that the fundamentalists wished to return to values of a former time, that is, to values prevalent as recently as the 50s and early 60s.

This response to the fundamentalists was not surprising. Those who have recently succeeded in legitimizing a new set of values tend to regard those they have recently left behind as retrograde or worse. And the fundamentalists presented some of these "outdated" values in a particularly sharp and angular fashion. But the response was exaggerated beyond reason. Not only were particular positions advocated by the fundamentalists rejected, so were the means they used to broadcast those positions. These techniques, however, though not always genteel, are perfectly appropriate to our political system. And they will have lasting political resonance only if they first resonate favorably within the consciousness of a considerable number of American citizens. The outraged response was particularly strange coming from religious groups that had long employed similar means to promote their own particular views on social issues. The crucial difference, apparently, was whose sheep were being shepherded--and in what direction.

* * *

No less than other religious communities, the Jewish communities have been reconsidering traditional positions and alliances. Some of their shifts are related to those that have taken place among Catholics and Protestants. For example, many liberals in this country, particularly those who moved toward a radical left, have developed sympathies for Third World revolutionaries and their goals. In some instances this has led them to support not only the rights of the Palestinian people, but the Palestine Liberation

Religion

Organization (PLO) and, consequently, to an attentuation of their former strong sympathies for Israel. Some longstanding ties are further strained when those who see the need for an enhanced military establishment--both for the U.S. and for Israel--support new military measures that some liberals reject. Such political reorientations have led to a weakening of former established ties with some Christian organizations.

At the same time, and exactly on these issues, Fundamentalists and some evangelicals offer themselves as political allies to the Jewish community. That the religious right in the country has a residual history of being racist, anti-Catholic, and anti-Semitic is not overlooked, nor are some of the highly conservative stands they take on a number of domestic issues, but there are now grounds for dialogue that were previously absent. And a number of people argue that as the religious right becomes more of a national political force they will, as almost all such groups do, tend to move toward the political center.

Although attitudes toward Israel remain crucial in the Jewish community, there are other domestic political factors at play today. It was taken for granted not long ago that, on most social issues, the Jewish community would have a left-liberal orientation. This expectation must now be moderated, as are some of the positions taken by prominent Jewish organizations and leaders.

* * *

This necessarily schematized view of our present religious scene has, admittedly, some depressing aspects although, also admittedly, not all observers will be depressed by the same aspects. But it also has some exhilarating prospects. In the past, religious conflict in this country could best be understood by examining differences between Catholics, Protestants and Jews, as each group tried to live by and transmit its vision to American life. Now these religious communities, while maintaining their distinct identities, increasingly work together on matters of common interest. Religious differences can now better be understood as a matter of cross alignments, liberals and radicals within different religious groups pitted against the conservatives within those groups on a wide range of issues. But these forces are not neatly drawn. The alliances shift as they move from one issue to another, illustrating almost to a fault the essential pluralism of this country.

No overview of religion as a factor in our pluralistic society would be complete without reference to the efforts of the Supreme Court to cope with religion. We begin with the melancholy fact that the Court's attempts to define religion over the last several decades are a very model of disorder. In its decisions concerning the "free exercise" of religion the Court has enlarged the meaning of the term religion so that it embraces nonbelievers as well as believers, and what in ordinary parlance would be understood as philosophy rather than religion. The process of elasticizing "religion" began in 1947, when Justice Black, writing in the Everson decision, rejected earlier Court definitions and explicitly referred to "nonbelievers" as a category to be given equal status with Methodists, Presbyterians, Jews, Catholics and other traditional theistic religions. The process of stretching the definition of the term has continued and it would be a bold prophet who would attempt to predict if and when it will cease. But some of the consequences are clear. As the term is extended to encompass more "religious" groups, the distinctive meaning and value of the "free exercise" provision diminishes.

In its decisions concerning the "no-establishment"

Religion

provision, however, the Court has tended to define "religion" more narrowly, so that traditional religions operate under more constraints than do the marginal, cultish or "philosophic" religions. In practice this means that in the Court's attempt to maintain separation of church and state, to see that the government does not advance any religion, theistic religions come under particularly close scrutiny. The results are apparent. In our school systems, for example, traditional religions are rigorously (but sometimes inconsistently) excluded, while other definable value-systems have free entry. At its ludicrous, though serious, extreme educators and textbook writers--fearful of being accused of bringing religion into the public schools--provide textbooks from which one could not learn that the initial settlers or the founding fathers of this country had any interest in religion, and in which Christmas is defined as a warm occasion on which good food is served. The practical consequence of such contradictory rulings, according to a number of critics, is that the Supreme Court of the United States has become neutral *against* religion.

These critics point out--what is open to common observation--that public places, ceremonies and offices are gradually being denuded of religious reference. They further point out--what does not receive common agreement--that to omit references to religion is not to teach nothing about it; it is to teach that religion is at best of secondary importance, a matter of private but not public concern. This is not, the critics conclude, what the founders of this country intended, what the Constitution stipulates, or what most Americans want.

These issues are serious, as are people on both sides of the debate. Religious believers who participate in this debate must do so within the framework established by our political processes, relying on the same grounds of evidence and reason available to those who do not share their beliefs. But they must not be excluded from the public forum (as some who are opposed to their views now argue) because they speak and act out of religious motivation.

The time is not yet discernible when we will cease to be a country of many diverse, rich subcultures, each protecting its own set of values and attempting to communicate them by precept and example to the general culture. Among the influential subcultures, those of religious communities are not negligible, and the debates to which I have alluded will be with us for some time. For the separation of church and state was never intended to be--and in this country cannot be--a separation of religion and society. Today, our subcultures, including notably those of religion, present in a new form a long-standing American question: How much unity do we need, how much diversity can we stand? It remains a glory of the American experience that our political processes allow our various subcultures to participate actively, constantly checking excesses of other competing visions even as they make valuable contributions of their own.

Marxism-Leninism: Implications for the United States

Paul Seabury

Much has changed since the days of the Second World War. But there is an important political-military thread of continuity which links those times to ours in a very important fashion. Then and now, the Soviet Union was and is informed in its fundamental strategic view of the world by doctrines derived from Lenin. These Leninist tenets permeate its strategic planning.

For various reasons, Americans have not taken Marxism-Leninism seriously for a long time. This is true even of many experts who consider the Soviet challenge to be serious, affecting our very survival as a free society. At the risk of oversimplification, I would claim that many quite well-informed Americans, hardened to the realities of the Soviet "empire" and its activities, have come around to the view that Marxist-Leninist ideology has simply degenerated into a rigid system of enforced belief administered by authorities who have no particular commitment to it other

Marxism-Leninism

than to employ it in order to remain in power. In this regard, "Marxism" (like "God" in America of the 1960s) is deemed "dead," surviving only in the publicity offices of formal establishments as a means of maintaining their authority. Marxism-Leninism is thought to be no different from the moribund "divine right of kings," which undergirded the monarchical establishments of seventeenth century Europe.

Oddly enough, the "socialism-is-dead" theme is found today in the writings of such prominent American neoconservatives as Irving Kristol, George Gilder and many others. It is also echoed in Europe in the writings of such eminent philosophers as Leszek Kolakowski of Poland and Paul Johnson of England.

* * *

There is another reason why Marxism-Leninism is not taken seriously in the United States. For all of its powerful aspects as an operational weapon, it has been rationally rejected in all of its parts. Since it has been so long at the service of the *nomenklatura* of the Soviet Union, who employ it as a weapon against us, the unrelenting incantation of its dogmas has dulled our interest in it. The effect of this ceaseless bombardment has been to turn our attention from it, if only to preserve our sanity; overexposure to it can have exactly the same dulling effect as it has upon those who are comdemned to live under Soviet rule. Life, with its wonders, is too short to take Marxist-Leninist ideology seriously as an "objective" fact of our existence. Thus, the suggestion that there actually are those who do take it seriously is not taken seriously.

One is reminded of the historical fact that almost no one in the United States in the 1930s took seriously Hitler's ideology, laid out in *Mein Kampf.* The unexpurgated version of that volume never appeared in English translation until 1939. By then, the hour was late. The writings of the Ayatollah Khomeni, widely disseminated in Farsi in the 1970s, did not appear in English until 1980 and I doubt that many Americans have yet bothered to consult them. And, of course, one might wonder how many intelligent Westerners have ever seen, much less read, Qadhafi's official Green Book, another tract of our times. Such is the regnant power of our own Western, liberal system of beliefs that we relegate these foolishnesses to trash bins.

To take these beliefs seriously as fundamental threats to ourselves, is to risk being regarded as paranoid. The long plague upon anticommunism (known as anti-anticommunism) is an important fact of comtemporary Western intellectual life. The relationship between confidence and complacency is always ambiguous, but never more so than today.

There is also a fear that a concern about Marxism-Leninism will lead to a perverse, emulative mirror-imaging. To take it seriously, many argue, would be also to advocate a negative and repugnant ideology, subversive of our liberal democratic institutions. An early victim of this criticism was Whitaker Chambers; a more recent one, Solzhenitzyn; a most recent one, Sakharov. Yet these individuals stand in a long tradition; one need only recall from the early war years the powerful warning of Hermann Rauschning, the Nazi defector, who, in his *Revolution of Nihilism* described the inner nature of national socialism.

Thus, the difficult, paradoxical challenge is how to take dangerous ideas seriously without taking them seriously. Westerners are too often outraged by the excesses of inhumane regimes without bothering to explore the ideas which give rise to them in the first place. Such organizations as Amnesty International, it seems to me, illustrate the point:

by focusing exclusively upon inhumanities *per se,* they cover their eyes to the differing worlds of political ideas that inspire them. Thus, they indiscriminately lump together those whose inhumanities are of an age-old nature with those whose inhumanities are consequences of all-too-contemporary ideologies. One cannot understand our times without admitting that Pol Pot, whose Khmer Rouge in 1975 exterminated perhaps twenty percent of the Cambodian population, is a child of our times, a former Sorbonne student, and not an atavistic throwback to an older barbaric era.

And our thoughts about terrorism are often similarly flawed. Many tend to address the problem of meeting terrorism tactically, in concrete situations, while ignoring its deeper, ideational origins. Americans particularly tend to accept the benign view that revolutionary developments in Central America, for example, spring somehow from our own failure to understand the "indigenous" roots of revolt and rebellion, ignoring the specifically modern ideas which inform and control these movements.

* * *

I propose to treat the central topic of this paper by responding to two questions. *First,* in what ways does Marxism-Leninism inform the specific military-combative aspect of our chief adversaries, contributing to their strategic and tactical dispositions toward us and toward others of their avowed enemies? *Second,* in what ways does Marxism-Leninism as philosophy and action-strategy affect our strategic defense policies in areas other than that of our direct confrontation with the Soviet Union? While the first of these questions is certainly the more important one, I think its broad outlines are such that I need only sketch them.

In the "good old days," as far as the United States was concerned, this particular challenge was not very important. Until World War II, the Soviet Union was certainly not more than a huge regional power. Its military capacities were deployed toward geographic areas immediately adjacent to it. This is not to denigrate that power; before 1939, the USSR already occupied most of what the British geopolitician Halford Mackinder referred to as the "heartland." It loomed over Europe; it had great capacities. But, at that time, few aside from Stalin's immediate neighbors, and its own inhabitants, had much reason to fear it as a military power. By 1938, in fact, the general tendency in the West (and in Nazi Germany as well) was to denigrate Soviet military capacities. The fear of the Soviet Union in the West was not so much fear of its military capabilities (who, in the 1930s stayed up nights fearing that Soviet tanks would smash westward to the English Channel?) as of its looming presence as an ideological force with strong allies in the Communist parties in the West. The United States at that time had perhaps the least to fear from this power. Russia was very far away and communism had little appeal in the U.S., even in the depression; the Soviet armed forces, even in the eyes of U.S. military observers, were not highly regarded. (In early 1941, when Operation Barbarossa broke forth, U.S. military experts gave the Red Army only a few weeks before it would break under the weight of the German *Reichswehr*.)

* * *

Soviet views about the relationship between war and politics were and still are a radical readaptation of the views of Karl von Clausewitz (1780-1831) the great Prussian strategic thinker. It was Clausewitz who coined the aphorism

Marxism-Leninism

that war is a continuation of politics by an admixture of other means. It was Lenin who reversed the dictum: politics is a continuation of war by an admixture of other means. In the Soviet view then and now, in strategic matters both in times of fighting and nonfighting, the Soviet Union is always necessarily at war; politics is not just a *particular* aspect of the general art of warfare--politics *is* war. Therefore, the formal distinction usually drawn by Western nations between times of war and times of peace is--in Soviet eyes--not a valid one.

Politics is a friend-foe relationship. This idea, not novel in world history, is nevertheless diametrically at odds with Western views which regard peace not just as the absence of fighting but as a time when the friend-foe relationship should have no meaning. In this regard, the Marxist-Leninist view of contemporary world history as class conflict on a global scale takes on particular meaning. Even in the so-called phase of detente of the 1970s, the Soviets never abandoned this framework.

The Clausewitz/Lenin view, imbedded in Soviet doctrine, provides a strategic starting point for an analysis and understanding of international relations. Realists in the West--a minority at odds with the dominant, liberal view of world politics--have depicted international relations as a balance of power. This view, too, is competitive and rivalrous. But such a world view differs fundamentally from the Leninist one: the realists' "balance" is inherently nonideological, arising from tensions among the interests and security concerns of individual nations, concerns which are essentially the same for all nations. The Leninist equivalent of the balance of power is a doctrine called the "correlation of forces" (*sootnoshenie sil*), a standard by which the Soviet Union at all times measures its own forces and those of its allies against its necessary and inevitable ideological enemies--the capitalist world and the *chief* capitalist enemy, the United States. This view is indeed a far cry from original Marxist, pre-Leninist views of politics, which saw the contemporary class struggle as inherently a passing aspect of the inner polities of advanced industrial states. It is now largely forgotten that Marx and Engels' emphasis on class conflict did not lead them to employ it (as Lenin later did) as a theory of international politics and war. Lenin transposed the conflict into encounters among states; contemporary Soviet theory continues this tradition. But as Engels wrote a century ago:

> The entire danger of a world war will vanish on the day when a change of affairs in Russia will permit the Russian people to put an end to its tsars' traditional policy of conquest and attend to its own vital interests...instead of to fantasies of world conquest.

The world view of the correlation of forces translates international conflict into a dichotomy between the Soviet Union (and its proxies and satellites) and the West. Further, and most importantly, this world view, in the eyes of many Western observers, is one in which the Communist/Leninist element, for all practical purposes, is now virtually indistinguishable from that of the Soviet state and from that of Russian imperialism, a phenomenon which long antedates the Bolshevik Revolution.

This view, though it is advocated by some Western observers, must be severely qualified in order to have any credibility. If we observe all of those Communist states which are Communist "in their own right," and not simply Soviet satrapies such as the Eastern European countries, we note the ubiquitous manifestations of the Clausewitz-Leninist view. If war and politics are indistinguishable, then it follows that the Marxist-Leninist state must at all times be thoroughly militarized, vigilant and equipped with huge forces-in-being prepared for combat both at home and abroad.

Thus, wherever one looks in the world today for great military garrison states, one looks almost exclusively at the Communist world. The armed forces of North Korea, considered as men-under-arms, exceed those of the United States; the Cuban army is the largest in Latin America; the army of Communist Vietnam exceeds the U.S. Army in numbers by nearly half a million; the army of Nicaragua under the Sandinistas is larger than those of all its neighbors combined, and is four times the number of Canadian soldiers. The plans of the Communist New Jewel Movement in Grenada, before that regime collapsed, were to mobilize as much as 25 percent of the Grenadian population. And, of course, this is before we begin to count noses of the Red Army in the Soviet Union, the forces of the other Warsaw Pact nations, and the People's Liberation Army of China.

* * *

We should disabuse ourselves of the notion that Marxism-Leninism represents a threat to us only because it is wedded to Soviet and Soviet/Russian imperial propensities: the threat is more serious than that. As a worldview and an operational code, it is now accepted by all major Communist states and by many other states in the pro-Soviet parts of the Third World. In these states, military power at all times is Janus-headed: the enemy is both within and without; military and paramilitary forces are guardians of the state against external enemies and their own populations.

At the beginning of the long contest between the Communist world and ours in the 1940s, the West, and America in particular, was able to maintain its overall strategic preeminence by virtue of its commanding lead in high technology and fire power. In the early years of the Cold War, for instance, the Soviet capacity to project military power was strictly limited to regions immediately adjacent to it in Europe and the Far East. The United States could and did accept numerical inferiority in conventional forces because of this fact. The United States and its NATO allies, in designing their European theater forces, adopted what might be called a "capital intensive" system of forces-in-being, juxtaposed to a Soviet "labor intensive" force. This led the West to introduce nuclear forces into Europe at a time when the Soviets were not yet able to reciprocate in kind. In Korea, we saw (as we later would see in Vietnam) a war in which the Communist side deployed huge forces of combat soldiers, while the other side deployed significantly smaller numbers with greater fire power and more sophisticated technology. In both wars, the Communists accepted gigantic battlefield losses in manpower, far greater than did its adversaries.

I mention these historical facts in order to point out that this original capital-intensive versus labor-intensive opposition made it possible, in part, for the United States and its allies to avoid "mirror imaging" their opponents by drafting huge armies. But, in time, the Soviets and their allies have rectified their side of the balance. In all or nearly all categories of sophisticated weaponry, they are now keen rivals of the West, and the Soviets can project their forces in distant parts of the globe where their presence was scarcely felt before. The overall comparability of the U.S. and the USSR in nuclear weaponry is now too familiar to warrant extended attention. The increasing dependence of the U.S. on ever more sophisticated and costly weaponry as a means of recovering its once unparalleled technological advantage has created severe logistical problems. For example, the

Marxism-Leninism

length of time required in 1980 from order to delivery of highly sophisticated U.S. fighter planes was almost exactly the length of time between Pearl Harbor and VJ-Day. The Soviet Union, with its enormous military forces, is now *both* capital and labor intensive.

* * *

As these observations suggest, the strategic implications of Marxist-Leninist ideology for established Communist states differs from its orignal role as a *movement* ideology. When it is institutionalized, the movement ideology becomes a weapon administered by the state to mobilize and control its people and to expand the range of the movement-state's power into other regions.

This matter of internal control is of seminal importance in any Communist state, and the military forces are a principle vehicle by which this control is cemented. Obviously, the armed forces provide a powerful weapon to directly control the population. They also serve as a means of indoctrinating youth into the proper ideological conformity, i.e., a means of transforming consciousness. Yet, the matter goes far beyond this into the doctrinal necessity to regard all forms of social, artistic and economic activity as combat. As the bishops of Nicaragua observed, in a pastoral letter of 29 August 1983, the Sandinista's then-proposed universal conscription law

> ...is strongly politicized in its fundamental points, it has a partisan character and it follows the general lines of all totalitarian legislation.
> ...The Military Service does not only 'promote the learning of the most advanced military techniques' (Consideration VII), but also 'will form in our youth the sense of *revolutionary* discipline and morality.' That is, the Army is

converted into an obligatory center of political indoctrination in favor of the Sandinista Party.... To force the citizens to join an 'Army-Political Party' without being in agreement with the ideology of said political party, is an act against the liberty of thought, of opinion, and of association. (Ref. Universal Declaration of the Rights of Man, arts. 18, 19 and 20.)

Does the ideology of the military/revolutionary Communist state differ essentially from the "movement" ideology? Yes and no. It differs in that its function is transformed into that of consolidating a totalitarian regime and subjugating a captured society. But it resembles the "movement" ideology in that the state becomes the "movement" and the "movement" is henceforth at the disposal of those who intend to employ it for the further revolutionary transformation of those still beyond its reach. This expansionist propensity has always been the case with truly revolutionary regimes. The French soldiers under Bonaparte, sweeping across Europe, carried the Declaration of the Rights of Man in their knapsacks. Cuban mercenaries in Africa and the Middle East are presumably indoctrinated with the Communist version of revolutionary romanticism.

It seems to me that the problem which the United States now faces in Central and South America and the Caribbean has been misunderstood by many influential Western leaders and opinion-makers. Not so long ago, the point was made by some distinguished critics of Reagan Administration policy that the *tumultos* (uprisings) of that region were matters somehow separable from the rivalries of East-West relations. This group, including such figures as Cyrus Vance, Edmund Muskie, David Rockefeller, General David Jones and Robert McNamara, stated:

> We all favor keeping Latin America and the Caribbean out of the East-West conflict to the greatest extent possible. It

does not serve the purpose for the United States to oppose changes in the region simply because they diminish U.S. influence and hence are perceived as advantageous to Cuba and the Soviet Union, unless they are clearly related to basic security concerns. We believe that the United States can better achieve its long-term interest in regional stability, one shared by Latin Americans, by exercising measured restraint in the projection of its power.

The sentiment expressed in this passage is shared by many well-meaning Westerners, but unfortunately the wish is rarely father to the reality. Often the wish is that reality correspond to policy, rather than the other way around. In *The Grenada Papers*, I document the extent to which that East-West conflict had permeated a tiny Caribbean island. Before the Bishop regime suddenly collapsed of internal contradictions, it had become a base for Soviet, Cuban, Bulgarian, East German, North Korean, Vietnamese and other Marxist-Leninist forces.

* * *

In Central America today, we encounter a conundrum: What is the nature of the relationship between the gigantic apparatus of Soviet-bloc state power, which sponsors these movements, and these intrahemispheric movements themselves? Here we encounter two opposed interpretations. Both, I emphasize, contain important elements of truth.

One is that these Central American *tumultos* are essentially products of Soviet strategic nurturing and that they therefore should be viewed as extensions by proxy of Soviet power in the Western Hemisphere, or even (as in El Salvador) as proxies of proxies. Seen in their totality, then, these movements would comprise a geographic aspect of a larger "correlation of forces," a part of a whole. If therefore, it is true, as Zbigniew Brzezinski said recently, that Soviet political-military strategy today concentrates not so much upon conquest of the West as upon its strategic destabilization and disruption, the specifically *military* implications of Central America (foward military, naval and air bases) are of far less importance than the *political*-military ones.

In this respect, the transformation of the whole region of the Caribbean, Central America and Mexico into a zone of hostile totalitarian regimes, or the degradation of the region into sociopolitical turmoil, would have equally damaging consequences for the overall strategic posture of the United States in the world. For more than a century and a half, since the Napoleonic Wars in fact, the United States has never been faced by powerful, hostile forces and states or social chaos in the Western Hemisphere. Were Marxist-Leninists to triumph in a series of victories in Central America, the symbolic importance surely would have profound effects in Mexico. The United States, faced by a large, hostile or profoundly destabilized Mexico directly on its border, would be compelled to direct its attention away from other crucial regions of the world in order to face this ominous challenge on its doorstep.

* * *

It is here that a second interpretation of these hemispheric events must be carefully considered: that the events themselves are not so much strategic exports of the Soviet Union, as they are *indigenous* Marxist-Leninist developments. In this interpretation, these forces (which also include Maoists and Trotskyites among their ranks) arise spontaneously, having been inspired by strands of Marxist-Leninist thought which have existed in the Western Hemi-

Marxism-Leninism

sphere for a very long time. This process does not necessarily require nor is it necessarily dominated by the experiences of Marxist-Leninist regimes elsewhere. One important inspiration to regional Marxism-Leninism arises from a hatred of Yankee North America, born of an admixture of envy and contempt. In this regard, many Americans fail to realize that the chief intellectual center of Marxism-Leninism in the Western Hemisphere is not Havana, but *Mexico City*, and that idiosyncratic Latin characteristics of these revolutionary Communist movements predates the Second World War. Until now, the governing party of Mexico (the PRI) has hosted and tolerated these forces inside its borders, warily professing its revolutionary credentials by evincing sympathy for revolutionary causes as long as the sites of battle are *outside* Mexico.

The PRI's self-proclaimed status as an authentic revolutionary political order, however, is now proving a somewhat mixed blessing. Its sympathy for "progressive forces" at work in areas adjacent to it is increasingly mixed with fear that the success of those forces may spill over into Mexico itself. Its support and toleration of truly Marxist-Leninist forces abroad is a form of calculated appeasement. Given the grave social problems which Mexico now faces, one must assume that Mexican political stability is not to be taken for granted.

It would be dangerously wrong to regard the vitality of Marxism-Leninism in this region only as an extension of Soviet strategic operations. Leszek Kolakowski, the Polish intellectual who has pronounced Marxism-Leninism as "dead" in his country and in Eastern Europe as a whole, would be hard put to pronounce it dead in the Western Hemisphere.

The common denominator of all Marxist-Leninist groups in Central America, as Michael Radu pointed out, has been "their open, consistent, and deeply felt belief that the United States is their main enemy....The realization that external support necessary to conquer power would come only from the USSR and its satellites was the necessary corrollary of a rapidly spreading conviction...that victory required a regional and ultimately global perspective that put aside doctrinal differences."

It would be myopic to reduce the importance of these regional Marxist-Leninist movements to a sterile debate as to whether they are primarily indigenous or primarily nurtured by Soviet strategy. The sources of hatred and animosity toward democracy, the free enterprise system and the United States in particular, are not confined to these two sources. To refer once more to the Grenada documents, what is striking is the *range* of material and spiritual support which flowed into that tiny island, and the degree of affinity which the New Jewel Movement found with movements and radical states far removed from itself. This moral and material help came not only from Cuba and the Soviet Union and its satellites, but from such diverse places as North Korea, Vietnam, Libya (a principal supplier), Syria, Algeria, Iran and Iraq, and the P.L.O. and other terrorist organizations.

The curious relationship between "progressive" Marxist-Leninist revolutionary ideologues and atavistic non-Western religious fanatics needs to be explored. There are paradoxes here: on the one hand, the "progressives" and the "atavists" are united in a common hatred of Western constitutionalism, democracy and capitalism; yet from a strategic perspective the atavists are clearly dependent as prote`ge`s upon the power of their "modern" allies and sponsors. The hatred of Western culture surely will continue indefinitely, but its symbiotic alliance with Marxism-Leninism is a marriage of convenience. This marriage will flourish as long as both continue to regard the West, and America in particular, as weak and/or irresolute.

What is the significance of this world-wide network? It seems to me that its significance lies in a generalized hostility to the West which extends beyond the confines of Marxist-Leninist movements and states. All of these anti-Western movements think that they would benefit from the strategic weakening of the United States. The most effective means of paralyzing the United States as a global force is to confront it with insurmountable problems in its own backyard, thereby crippling its capacity to sustain its friends and allies elsewhere.

When the doctrine of containment was embraced by the United States in the early Cold War years, it focused upon containing the Soviet Union. There was no need then to deal with the strange network of Soviet surrogates which we now confront. In dealing with this burgeoning network as it affects the Western Hemisphere, we see that the multiplicity of forces arrayed against the United States in Central America have not been opposed by an equal, countervailing opposition. America's European allies are indifferent to her regional difficulties; the many friends of civic freedom throughout the world observe these events passively; and Americans are divided among themselves as to the severity of the danger and manner in which it should be countered. Many people who hold no illusions about the implications of Marxist-Leninist incursions into the Western Hemisphere are nevertheless demoralized into inaction by the seeming "inevitability" of their success. There is no necessary reason why this should be so. A primary future task of American foreign policy should be to forge coalitions of friendly and democratic forces which would join in containing and repulsing these incremental encroachments on the free world, whether they occur in Central America or elsewhere.

The Promise of National Restoration

Morton M. Kondracke

America has seldom seemed more free and secure than it is in 1986. Even in the 1950s, the last era of a general calm and prosperity, there was reason to fear the possibility of war with the Soviet Union and a chill in civil liberties at home. The United States was still divided, in principle, on the issue of racial equality. There was confidence in President Eisenhower, but an alienation was developing among American elites. The 1960s and 70s were periods of dislocation--an assassinated president, four "failed" presidencies, a lost war, any number of raucous "liberations," two major and several minor confrontations with the Soviet Union, energy crises-- culminating in a serious loss of confidence in the capacity of the government to cope with the nation's problems.

The day after he lost the 1980 election, President Carter said that "inexorable forces of history" made it impossible for any president to do any better than cope.

National Restoration

Even before the election, Carter aide Lloyd Cutler had written in *Foreign Affairs* that constitutional changes creating a quasi-parliamentary system were necessary to enable a president to govern. Economic insecurity caused by high inflation, interest rates and unemployment led influential commentators to wonder whether our "postindustrial economy" could ever again provide growth and opportunity for the citizenry. They feared that the future of American politics and economics would consist of "zero sum" combat over shrinking resources.

* * *

President Reagan has restored the nation's morale. He has demonstrated that a president can govern effectively under our 200-year-old Constitution, can get programs through Congress even if they are controversial, and can conduct an assertive foreign policy. It remains to be seen whether the president's major policies--especially his economic policies--have been as wise as they have been politically successful.

Mr. Reagan's devotion to free market economics and lower taxes has not produced an increase in American savings, investment, productivity or average family income. If a prolonged recession occurs, whether brought on by excessive federal debt, by a world banking crisis or by America's inability to compete in international trade, it could once again shake the nation's confidence in itself. When Americans do not have faith that the whole of the nation can advance together, they are tempted to use political influence to protect themselves as members of special interest groups, at the expense of other groups and of the whole. At the moment, this is only a potential source of danger. At the moment, the 1980s hold the promise of being seen in

American history as a golden moment of national restoration.

* * *

That is so for most Americans, but certainly not for all. Thirty-four million Americans live below the poverty line. An estimated 20 million are undernourished and perhaps 2 million are homeless. The problem is more acute for children than adults--one-fifth of all U.S. children live in poverty, one-sixth of whites, 40 percent of Hispanics and 50 percent of blacks. While America has solved the problem of racial inequality on the legal level and has made strides toward economic equality for middle class blacks--those with college educations now earn as much as their white counterparts--there is still a wide disparity between the net worth of black and white families. The average white family owns property worth $39,135, whereas the black median is $3,397, trailing Hispanics, who have $4,913. Below even the median, the black underclass is growing and is presenting the nation with a seemingly insoluble burden of dependency, misery and crime. If there is hope, it lies in a new dedication to self-reliance within the black community, but their problems are deep-seated: 44 percent of all black families are headed by women (*vs.* 13 percent for whites) and half of all black babies are born out-of-wedlock (*vs.* 12 percent for whites). A white male has a one-in-131 chance of being murdered; for blacks, the figure is one-in-21.

The Reagan administration claims that it is assisting the black trend toward self-help and decreased reliance on government programs, but polls show that black leaders and black citizens believe the administration is unfriendly to them. Not only have benefit programs for the poor been cut back, but the Reagan Justice Department has vigorously opposed expansion of civil rights remedies in voting rights and affirmative action. The U.S. Supreme Court has rejected administration policy on both counts, dismissing with special decisiveness the administration claim that only specific victims of discrimination can be accorded favorable job treatment under affirmative action. It is debatable whether hiring and promotion quotas and other devices for "reverse discrimination" benefit blacks in the long run. The administration may well be right that affirmative action sustains dependency and leads both blacks and whites to wonder whether blacks who advance have done so on the basis of merit or government favoritism. That case might be heard more sympathetically by blacks if the administration showed any sympathy toward them. As it is, administration policies seem to have perpetuated the sense of alienation that many blacks feel toward their government.

* * *

The administration is also accused of being "repressive" because it stands, at least rhetorically, for government intervention in such social issues as abortion, protection for seriously handicapped newborns and the availability of contraception to minors. It also favors action to combat pornography and has embarked on several well-publicized campaigns to stop leaks of sensitive information to the press.

In action, the administration has presented a far less menacing threat to rights of privacy and free expression than its critics allege, and nothing like the threat posed by government in earlier periods in American history. The administration does intend, if possible, to secure reversal of the *Roe v. Wade* decision, which established broad legal rights to abortion. However, it has virtually abandoned hopes of making abortion illegal nationwide by constitutional amendment. It hopes, rather, to return to the separate states the decision to determine under what conditions abortion might be allowed. The Supreme Court has found that homosexual sodomy is not a constitutionally protected right under the rubric of privacy, but there is no impulse on the part of the government to encourage prosecution of homosexuals.

In the area of free expression, the Justice Department has sponsored a Commission on Pornography which recommended making trafficking in obscene material a felony and which urged stores to stop carrying mildly salacious magazines. The latter is a questionable activity being challenged in court, but there seems no disposition on the part of the federal government to launch a prosecutorial crusade against any but child pornography. Rather, the commission's actions can be seen as an attempt by conservatives to express displeasure with the surfeit of sexually explicit material available to the public.

In the area of press censorship for national security purposes, the Director of Central Intelligence has threatened to prosecute news organizations responsible for printing secrets whose disclosure he deems damaging to the national interest. However, no prosecutions actually have taken place and none is likely. The government has used polygraphs to determine whether its own officials are responsible for leaks, and has fired a few employees. This may be viewed, however, as an attempt to restore within the bureaucracy discipline that had badly deteriorated during the 1960s and 70s. Such efforts have had little effect in stemming the flow of information reaching the press.

A greater danger than press disclosures, however, is the loss of secrets to the Soviet bloc through espionage and theft, which represents a long-term threat to the freedom of

National Restoration

the American people. The government has been severely embarrassed by a spate of spy cases suggesting that its security services are woefully inadequate in clearing persons who are to have access to classified material and conducting counter-espionage investigations to protect secrets. The administration at one point was tempted to impose draconian restrictions requiring former high-level officials to clear every piece of writing for life with the government. Under pressure from Congress, the administration wisely thought better of the proposal.

* * *

In terms of the use of government power to stifle dissent or freedom of the press, this period in no way resembles the Kennedy, Johnson or Nixon eras, when the FBI, CIA and Internal Revenue Service allegedly were used routinely to investigate and harrass political adversaries. During that period there developed an attitude that presidents and their key advisers were fully justified in using foreign intelligence methods--wiretaps, break-ins, surveillance--against domestic opponents. The lasting importance of the Nixon Watergate scandal does not lie in the details of that administration's wrongdoing. Rather, it is this: The nation had to put a stop to excessive use of the national security apparatus by administrations in general. President Nixon may not have been the worst presidential malefactor. *Some* President had to be stopped to serve as an example for all others, and it was he. There is no justification for allegations that the Reagan administration represents a return to pre-Watergate tendencies.

What seems to be happening, rather, is a general scaling back across the board on the excesses of 1960s and 70s "liberation." In the Vietnam/Watergate era, it became routine for public officials to leak classified information for the purpose of promoting or sabotaging government policy. The Reagan administration has attempted a modest restoration of discipline. It has succeeded only modestly, primarily because some of its highest officials merely preach discretion, but do not practice it.

In social life, the restoration of middle-class values has come about heavily by popular demand in this overwhelmingly middle-class country. Sometimes, it has even been encouraged by former liberationists themselves. Feminists, for example, have come to see pornography as the exploitation of women for the gratification of men. Some of them have advocated censorship, and they have had to be restrained by the courts. Sexual promiscuity has led to an increase in venereal disease, including deadly AIDS. While more liberal divorce laws served the purpose of preventing harmful and expensive court battles, it is also clear that easy divorce has worked to the economic detriment of women. The women's liberation movement did the service of opening up careers previously denied to women; on the other hand, it also created a climate in which women were forced by social pressure to be employed rather than remain in the home. Now feminists are becoming increasingly aware that child rearing is an important activity for women to be engaged in.

There is some danger that right-wing extremists could threaten liberty in America. They seek in some states, for example, to expunge evolution from biology books and "secular humanism" from literature. However, there is constantly a contest for cultural dominance in American life, and currently the balance still favors liberal enlightenment, perhaps even to excess. A number of writers have noted, for example, that religion has been so completely expunged from the nation's schoolbooks that American children are denied information about the important roles that religious figures have played in the history of the nation.

* * *

Without representing a threat to liberty, the growing importance of money in politics does represent a threat to the idea of equal representation for all persons within their government. It is clear that property has always managed to speak with force in the government--and the more property, the more force. It is also true that campaign reform laws passed in the wake of Watergate have required disclosure of the receipts and disbursements of political candidates and special interest lobbies. However, the costs of running for office have exploded because of the need to buy television advertising. Candidates for office--including incumbent office-holders--are required to spend inordinate amounts of time and energy raising money. Those in possession of that money tend to be wealthy corporate interests with business they would like to do with the government. What has arisen, as a result, is massive purchase of "access" to legislators through political action committees.

This does not represent raw bribery--money given in return for a specific favor--but something akin to it. Members of powerful congressional committees routinely receive hundreds of thousands of dollars in campaign contributions from interest groups affected by the committee's work. Members who face weak opposition seldom refuse contributions; they use the money to help their friends and build up their own power. Members elected before 1980 actually may use their accumulated campaign treasury as a personal retirement fund. All of this is not less corrupt for being legal and openly reported on the public record. Rather, we simply have a system of legal and public corruption. It is one which lowers public confidence in the government and it is in need of reform. The health of the American system is such that "good government" does survive the system, as witness the passage of tax reform in spite of the influence of special interest lobbies. The fundamental strength of the system is such, too, that when the public becomes aware of the extent of corruption in the system, it demands reform and eventually gets it.

* * *

The external threats to American liberty--from the Soviet Union, assorted radical movements, rightist dictatorships and terrorist groups--seem marginally less ominous in 1986 than they have for a decade or more. No one should be complacent about those threats, but the combination of forcefulness on the part of the Reagan administration and a sense of restraint imposed upon it by Congress have tended to produce a moderate and pragmatic foreign policy that protects American interests.

The United States is bargaining with the Soviet Union with a sense of strength and self-confidence that it did not have under previous administrations. The Reagan administration contributed to that strength--creating, for example, the Strategic Defense Initiative--but Congress created pressure for negotiation. The Reagan administration demonstrated willingness to use force to defend American interests, but Congress created pressure for American power to be used to advance democracy--most notably, in Central America--rather than simply to oppose communism.

Still, the United States does not have a truly bipartisan foreign policy. There is no firm consensus on what America should do about the most pressing foreign policy problems. The Democratic Party, if left to its natural impulses, would

National Restoration

probably allow the Sandinista regime in Nicaragua to consolidate its power and destabilize all of Central America. The Reagan administration, following its natural tendencies, might have invaded Nicaragua to overthrow the regime. A compromise has been worked out between clashing philosophies, and that pattern has repeated itself on issue after issue--South Africa, arms budgets, Soviet policy, the Philippines.

Undoubtedly the nation would have a more dependable and effective foreign policy if there were a true consensus. Defense budgeting could be conducted less wastefully and foreign powers would be less inclined to try to affect American public opinion. And yet, this is another instance where the system works--imperfectly and raucously, but works. In foreign or domestic policy, no one should be content to ignore America's imperfections. That is especially so where they damage lives or diminish respect for democracy. At the same time, in 1986, Americans deserve to respect their country. It offers opportunity. It promotes democracy. It guards liberty.

Contributors

Zbigniew Brzezinski was assistant to the president for National Security Affairs (1977-81) and is Herbert Lehman professor of government at Columbia University and senior adviser at Georgetown University Center for Strategic and International Studies. He is the recent author of *Game Plan: A Geostrategic Framework for the Conduct of the U.S.-Soviet Contest* (Atlantic Monthly Press, 1986) from which his included essay is adapted.

Leo Cherne was a cofounder and executive director of the Research Institute of America and vice-chairman of the President's Foreign Intelligence Advisory Board.

John Diebold is chairman and founder of The Diebold Group, Inc., an international management consultant firm based in New York. Diebold is also author of *Making the Future Work: Unleashing Our Powers of Innovation for the Decades Ahead* (Simon & Schuster, 1984), which was recently awarded the Freedoms Foundation medal.

James Finn is the editorial director of Freedom

Contributors

House. He has written a number of books, many articles and has lectured widely on the relation of religion to politics and culture.

Sidney Hook was for forty years professor of philosophy and chairman of the department at NYU, and is currently a senior research fellow at the Hoover Institution for War, Revolution and Peace, Stanford University. His present essay is an elaboration of an address delivered at SUNY, Stony Brook, Long Island in May 1984, and was published in the fall 1986 issue of *Contemporary Education*.

Max M. Kampelman, a Washington attorney, was for six years legislative counsel to Senator Hubert H. Humphrey, and is the chief U.S. negotiator at the U.S.-USSR arms-control talks in Geneva.

Morton M. Kondracke, former Washington bureau chief of *Newsweek*, is a senior editor of the *New Republic*. He appears frequently on television political talk shows.

John W. Riehm was dean of the School of Law of Southern Methodist University and executive vice president of a law publisher before becoming senior vice president-administration of Thomas J. Lipton and Company.

Burns W. Roper, chairman of the Roper Organization, Inc. has also been president of the American Association for Public Opinion Research, and president of the Market Research Council.

Bayard Rustin, organizer of the historic 1963 March on Washington that paved the way for the 1964 Civil Rights Act, heads the A. Philip Randolph Educational Fund, and formerly was board chairman and president of the APR Institute.

Paul Seabury, professor of government at the University of California, Berkeley, was chairman of the faculty of the College of Letters and Science, and vice chairman of the State Department's Board of Foreign Scholarships. His included essay is derived from an article that appeared in *Social Philosophy & Policy* in 1985.

Leonard R. Sussman, executive director of Freedom House, writes frequently in the press and specialized journals here and abroad on issues in mass communication, particularly the free flow of information.

Philip van Slyck, as editor for the Foreign Policy Association, helped design its Great Decisions adult education program. He is president of the public-policy consultant firm that bears his name.

Index

abortion, Reagan administration position on, 164-65
academic freedom, 55-71
　Civil Rights Law in protection of, 70; confusion of propaganda with, 65-71; dangers to, 65-70; definition of, 55-56; duties and responsibilities regarding, 62-65; heresy as right of, 59-60; history of, 60-61; immunity of, 59-60; internal policing of, 63-65, 68-71; qualifications for, 58-59; right to, 57-59
Accuracy in Academia, 68-70
affirmative action, 36, 164
Afghanistan, 43-45
AFL-CIO, 38
AIDS, 75-77
America:
　attitude toward Marxism-Leninism, 145-48; attitude toward Soviet power, changes in, 149-50; business orientation of, 21, 24-25; church and state, 142-43; civil rights movement, 22-23, 28-34, 38; culture of, international attitudes toward, 19-23, 25; democratic process in, 13-15; democratic values of, 1-2, 4-7; Eastern Europe and, 47-52; economic changes in, 30-34; equal opportunity in, agenda for, 36-38; film in, 23-24; foreign policy vs. domestic policy, 15-16; freedom and liberty as values, 76-77; in international community, 10-13, 16-17, 20-21, 24-25; liberty, threats to, 166-70; materialism of, 20-22; middle-class values, resurgence of, 167; military power of, vs. Soviet Union, 152-54; misperception of U.S. foreign intelligence, 115-17, 127; national interest, 17-18; political system of, 13-14; popularity of, 41-42; Protestantism in, 132-34; religion in, importance of, 131; religious alliances, 140-41; Roman Catholicism in, 135-37; South America, antagonism of toward; 158-60; vs. Soviet Union, 3-4, 10, 14-15, 43-44, 46; World War II's effect on, 9-11
American Association of University Professors, 56, 61-63; Basic Statement of Principles, 61-63
American Society of Newspaper Editors (ASNE), poll on press credibility, 97
Amnesty International, 147-48
anti-anticommunism, 147
anti-Western stance, in academia 66-70
anti-West movements, 159-60
Augustinium dictum, 57

Babbit, George, 20
"balancing" of values, 3, 150
Benton, William, 90
Big Story: How the American Press and Television Reported and Interpreted the Crisis of TET 1968 in Vietnam and Washington (Freedom House), 6
Black, Hugo, 7, 141
Blacks:
　agenda for helping, 36-39; alienation of, toward

175

Index

Reagan administration, 163-64; civil rights movement of, 22-23, 28-34, 38; economic situation of, deteriorating, 27-28, 30-35; struggle for equal opportunity, 28-36; underclass, 34-35, 163-64; unemployment of, 30-32
Bradlee, Benjamin, 88
Brzezinski, Zbigniew, 157
Bureau of Labor Statistics, 112

capital-intensive vs. labor-intensive systems (U.S. vs. Soviet Union), 152-53
Casey, William, 88
Census Bureau, 11-12
Central America, 155-60
Chambers, Whitaker, 147
Chaplin, Charlie, 113
Chesterton, G. K., 131
Chiang Kai-shek, 86
civil liberties, status of, in America, 73-80
civil rights movement, 22-23, 28-34, 38
Clague, Ewan, 112-13
class struggle (Marxist-Leninist view), 150-51
Clausewitz, Karl von, 149-50; Clausewitz/ Lenin view of war and politics, 149-52
coexistence, 3
Cogley, John, 136
Cold War, 153
Commission on Pornography, 165
Commonweal, 135
computers, 107-14
benefits of data collection, 111-12; ethical and moral questions raised by, 108-11;' future optimism about, 113-14; infallibility of, 110; matching techniques of, 109, 111; privacy invaded by, 109, 111; ubiquitousness of, 107-108
consensual documents, 92-93
containment doctrine (Cold War), 160
"correlation of forces," 3, 150-51, 156
covert action, legitimization of, 126

Davis, Angela, 67
democracy, 13-15
freedom of press in, problems of, 96-97, 100-105; impact on foreign policy, 15-16; industrial, 27-28; intelligence in, 117-18; national commitment to, 38
"democratic journalism," 95
detente, 3
Dewey, John, 56
divorce, 74
Djilas, Milovan, 46
Douglas, William, 131
Ducross, Michael, 110

Eastern Europe, 47-52
economics:
agenda for revitalizing American, 36-38; international, 11-12; need for intelligence in, 127-28; problems in Black underclass, 27-28, 30-35
education, proposed federal reforms, 36-37

Engels, F., 151
equal opportunity, agenda for, 36-38
espionage, American, 165-66
Everson decision, 141

feminist movement, 167
Final Act of the 1975 Conference on Security and Cooperation in Europe, 93
First Amendment, 129
Foreign Affairs, 47
"A Free and Responsible Press" (Hutchins Commission Report), 99
freedom, complexity of, 4-5
Freedom House;
founding of, 1-2, 5-7; World War II, attitude toward American involvement, 9-10
freedom of religion, 129
freedom of the press:
conflicts in, 5-7; Hutchins Commission statement on, 98-101; "press responsibility," 81-82, 99-105; problems of, in democracy, 96-97, 100-105; vs. government censorship, 84-89, 92, 165-66; wartime restrictions on, 85-87
free expression, Reagan's attack on pornography's right to, 165
free market economy, in international arena, 24-25
free speech, 6-7
Free Speech Movement (Berkeley), 67
fundamentalism, 137-40

Gilder, George, 46
Gordon, Kermit, 112
Green Book (Qadhafi), 147
Grenada, 85
The Grenada Papers, 156, 159
Griffith, William, 47
"guided journalism" (Malaysia), 103-104

Harris survey of press credibility, 98
Helsinki Accords, 93
Helsinki process, 15, 93
Hitler, Adolf, 146-47
Holmes, Oliver Wendell, Jr., 6-7
homosexuality, changing attitude toward, 75-76, 78, 165
Hutchins, Robert, 98, 135
Hutchins Commission, 89, 98-101

India, attitude toward Soviet Union, 43-44
industrial democracy, 27-28; problems of, 28
Information Age, 82-83, 108; need for intelligence in, 123-24
information technology,
evolution of, 108-111 (*See also* computers)
intelligence, 115-128
American perception of U.S. foreign, 115-17, 127; economic vs. military, 127-28; purpose of, 117; role of press in reporting about, 87-89; symmetry with Soviet Union, 126; terrorism, fighting with, 119-21; uses of, 121-26
International Covenant on Civil and Political Rights, 91-92

176

Index

internationalism (in U.S.), 9
International Monetary Fund, 51
International Security Council, 119
interventionism (U.S.), 9
isolationism (U.S.), 9
Israel, American Jewish attitudes toward, 140

Jewish communities, 139-40
Johnson, Paul, 146
Jones, David, 155-56
journalism (*See* press)

Kennan, George, 126
Kennedy, John, 135
Kennedy, Robert, 112
KGB, 118, 126
Khmer Rouge, 148
Khomeini, Ayatollah, 147
Kirkpatrick, Jeane, 67
Knight News Service, 111
Kolakowski, Leszek, 146, 158
Kristol, Irving, 146

League of Nations, resolution regarding international journalism, 89
Lenin, 150
Lewis, Sinclair, 20
libel law, 92
Lichter, S. Robert, 132
Lovejoy, Arthur O., 56
Lynch, Charles, 86

MacKinder, Halford, 149
MacLeish, Archibald, 90
McGovern, George, 134
McNamara, Robert, 155-56
Maoists, 157
Mao Zedong, 86
Marxism-Leninism, 3, 116, 145-160; changes in, 149-51; indigenous developments of, in Western Hemisphere, 157-60; intelligence in, 117-18; news media and, 83-84, 94-95; strategic implications of, 154-55; war and peace, attitude toward, 149-52
mass media;
 effect on Soviet empire 48-49, 52-53; reporting on religion in America, 131-32
media elite, 131-32
Mein Kampf, 146-47
Mencken, H. L., 20
Mexico, 157-58
"mirror imaging," 147, 153
MITI, 128
Modern Times (Chaplin), 113
Mohamad, Mahathir, 103
movement ideology vs. military/revolutionary ideology (Soviet Union), 154-55
Mowrer, Edgar Ansel, 85
Mowrer, Paul Scott, 85
mujahedeen, 43-45
Murray, John Courtney, 136
Muskie, Edmund, 155-56

Muslims, attitude toward Soviet Union, 43-47

National Council of Catholic Bishops, 136-37
National Council of Churches, 133-34
National News Council, 100-101
A Nation Prepared: Teachers for the 21st Century (Carnegie Report), 37
Nazism, 2-3
Neonationalist Third World, doctrine of the press, 94-95
Neuhaus, Richard John, 137
neutralism, European, 125
New Jewel Movement, 152, 159
"new journalism," 94
New School for Social Research, Declaration of the Graduate School, 63-64
Nicaragua, bishops pastoral letter, 154-55
Nixon, Richard, 166
"no-establishment" provision (religion), 141-42
nomenklatura, 146
non-Russians in Russia, U.S. currying of, 52-55
nuclear weaponry, Soviet vs. U.S., 153-54
nudity, 74

Office of War Information, 86
Official Secrets Act (Malaysia), 104
oil prices, 121-22
O'Neill, Michael J. 105
Operation Barbarossa, 149
opinion polls, 73-80; changes in tolerance in U.S., 74-78; freedom as important American value, 76-77; influence in changing opinions, 79-80; value of, 80
Oretga, Daniel, 134
Ottoman Empire, comparison to Soviet system, 46

pacifism (U.S.), 9
Palestine Liberation Organization, 139-40
pastoral letter on war and peace (NCCB, 1983), 136-37
Patriotic Commentators' Association (Japan), 86
Patriotic Critics' Association (Japan), 86
Pearl Harbor, 10
Peterson, Theodore, 101
Poland, 50-52
pluralism (of U.S. democracy), 21, 25, 141
plurality, in news media, 99-100
political action committees, 168-69
politics, American:
 combined with religion, 130, 138-39; inappropriateness in university, 65-68; influence of money in, 168-69
Pol Pot, 148
poor, in America, 35, 37-38, 163
Pornography Commission, 78
press, 81-105
 censorship of, 84-89, 92, 165-66; communications revolution, effect of on, 83-84; focus on "today's story," 83; four models of, 101-102; intelligence and military secrets, role of, in reporting on, 87-89; international proposals re-

177

Index

garding, 89-93; loss of credibility of, 82, 87, 97-98; Marxist-Leninist dogma, 94; monopolies, 99-100; Neonationalist Third World doctrine, 94; responsibility of, 81-82, 99-105; self-policing of, 104-105; views of Western and American, 94-96, 99; wartime restrictions on, 85-87; World War II, effect on, 82-83
"press responsibility," 81-82, 99-105
privacy, danger to from computer Information Age, 108-109, 111
private data networks, 110-11
(*See also* computers)
propaganda, at universities, 65-68
Protestantism in America, changes in, 132-34
public opinion (*See* opinion polls)

Qadhafi, Muammar, 147

Radio Free Afghanistan, 45
Radio Free Europe, 48-49
Radio Liberty, 53
Radu, Michael, 158-59
Rauschning, Hermann, 147
Reagan, Ronald, 162-63
Reagan administration, 23-24, 28, 32, 111, 134; attitude toward Blacks, 163-64; foreign policy of, 169-70; "repressiveness" of, 164-67
Rehnquist, William H., 22
religion:
changes in, 132-40; combined with politics, 130, 138-39; definition of, 141-42; divisive influence of, 130-31; freedom of, 129; importance of, in America, 131; media coverage of, 131-32; Supreme Court and, 141-43
Revolution of Nihilism, 147
"rights vs. duties" philosophy 7
rights
"absolute," 6-7; academic freedom as a special right, 57-59; balancing of, 5-7; majority vs. minority, 6; to access to information, 81, 91, 95-96; to free expression, 81, 91; to heresy, 59-60
Riverside Church (NYC), 134
Rockefeller, David, 155-56
Roe v. Wade, 138, 164
Roman Catholicism, 134-37
Roosevelt, Eleanor, 2
Roosevelt, Franklin Delano, 2
Roper Poll, 76
Rothman, Stanley, 132
rule of reason, 5

Sakharov, Andrei, 147
Schenck v. United States, 6-7
Schramm, Wilbur, 101
schools, religion in, 142
Second Vatican Council, 135-36
"secular humanism," 138, 167
security issues, effects on East Europe, 50
sexual attitudes, changing, 74-76
Shanker, Albert, 37
Siebert, Fred S., 101

silicon chips, 108
Sinclair, Upton, 20
"socialism is dead" theme, 146
sodomy (Georgia laws), 78, 165
Solidarity, 51
Solzhenitsyn, Alexander, 147
South America, 155-56, 158-60
Soviet Union:
attitude of America and West toward, 149; Central and South America, influence in, 159-60; Eastern Europe, involvement with, 47-52; expansionism of, 46-47, 155-56; flouting of free press accords, 93; intelligence in, 117-18, 126; military power of vs. U.S., 152-54; news media, influence on, 84-85, 91; proxy nations, use of, 118-20; structural changes in, 124; territorial character of, 42-43; vs. U.S., 3-4, 10, 14-15, 43-44, 46; war and politics, attitude toward (Clausewitz/Lenin view), 149-52; war in Afghanistan, 43-45
"State Terrorism and the International System" (conference), 119-20
Statue of Liberty, 77
Stimson, Henry, 126
Strategic Defense Initiative, 169
Supreme Court, impact on religion, 141-43
Survey of Freedom, 1

technology, U.S. intelligence need for, 124-25
terrorism, 119-21, 148
Third World countries, 11-12, 38, 85
Times Mirror Company (poll on press credibility), 98
Tocqueville, Alexis de, 15-16, 20, 130
tolerance, changes in American, 74-76
Trotskyites, 157
truth:
challenges to objective, 66; mission of university, 62, 66; variations in, 56-57

unemployment, Black, 30-32
UNESCO, 82, 90-92
United Methodist Church letter, 137
United Nations, 11
United States-Soviet relationship, 43-46, 52-55
Universal Declaration of Human Rights (Article 19), 91
university, changing concept of (politicization of), 65-69

Vance, Cyrus, 155-56
Vietnam, news reporting about, 87

Wachtler, Sol, 6
war, effect on news media, 85-87
Warsaw Pact, 52
Washington Post, 87-88
Watergate, the press and, 87, 94, 166
Wilkie, Wendell L., 2, 12
The Wizard of Oz (banned in Tennessee), 78

youth rebellion (60s and 70s), 22-23